101 WET
PLAYTIME GAMES
AND ACTIVITIES

www.teachingexpertise.com/teachtoinspire

101 WET PLAYTIME GAMES AND ACTIVITIES

'Take time to play – it is the secret of perpetual youth.'

Anonymous

Thérèse Hoyle

This book is commissioned by Barbara Maines and George Robinson for Teach to Inspire, a series for Optimus Education.

Author:

Thérèse Hoyle

Designer:

Jess Wright

Cover image: ©istockphoto.com/valkr

Editors:

George Robinson and Barbara Maines

Copy Editor:

Mel Maines

Illustrator:

Philippa Drakeford

Printed by: CMP (UK) Ltd.

Registered Office: G3 The Fulcrum, Vantage Way, Poole, Dorset BH12 4NU

Registered Number: 299 7187

Published by Optimus Education: a division of Optimus Professional Publishing Ltd.

Registered Office: 33-41 Dallington Street, London EC1V 0BB

Registered Number: 05791519

Telephone: 0845 450 6407 Fax: 0845 450 6410

www.teachingexpertise.com

ISBN 978-1-906517-10-6

A CD-ROM is attached to the inside front cover and is an integral part of this publication.

Contents

Use of the CD-ROM

Many Teach to Inspire publications include CD-ROMs to support the purchaser in the delivery of the training or teaching activities. These may include any of the following file formats:

- PDFs requiring Acrobat v.3.
- Microsoft Word files.
- Microsoft PowerPoint files.
- Video clips which can be played by Windows Media Player.
- If games are included the software required is provided on the CD-ROM.

All material on the accompanying CD-ROM can be printed by the purchaser/user of the book. This includes library copies. Some of this material is also printed in the book and can be photocopied but this will restrict it to the black and white/greyscale version when there might be a colour version on the CD-ROM.

The CD-ROM itself must not be reproduced or copied in its entirety for use by others without permission from the publisher.

All material on the CD-ROM is © Hoyle 2009

Symbol Key

 This symbol indicates a page that can be photocopied from the book or printed from the PDF file on the CD-ROM. The book title appears on the page in the book but not on copies printed from the CD-ROM.

 Thinking Games

 Paper Play and Technology Challenges

 Quiz and Puzzle Activities

 Circle Games

 Parachute Games

 Active Games for Letting Off Steam

 Singing, Rhymes and Dancing Games

Dedication

This book is dedicated to my mother, Jane Hoyle, who is an inspiration, guiding light and a beautiful, wise soul. Thank you for always believing in me.

Thérèse Hoyle is an educational consultant, trainer, author, teacher, leadership coach and motivational speaker. She offers professional support to schools and organisations nationally and internationally on such topics as positive playtimes, Circle Time, Social and Emotional Aspects of Learning, behaviour management, whole-school emotional literacy, wellbeing, values education, leadership and coaching. She is a sought after speaker at workshops and conferences nationally and internationally.

For further information contact:

therese@thesuccesspartnership.org

www.thesuccesspartnership.org

Acknowledgments

I would like to say an enormous thank you to all the children, teachers, head teachers, lunchtime supervisors and parents who have shared in the development of this work.

A special thank you goes to the schools and local education authorities I have worked in, particularly the cluster of nine schools I worked with in South Dunedin, New Zealand, running my Positive Playtime, Circle Time, Coaching/Mentoring and Turn a Round programmes over a two-year period. The result of their hard work and dedication speak for themselves, with a recent turnaround in the behaviour in the schools resulting in more engaged children and better learning. Musselborough School in particular has had a huge reduction in stand downs, which have gone from eight in 2006 to one in 2008.

'We had a neighbour say to us that our playground was different. She said you could hear there was a different atmosphere – it sounded happier.' Brent Caldwell, head teacher.

Thank you for all your hard work, trialling the many games and letting me test them out on the children too. In the UK, thank you too to the teachers and principal Sue Roberts of Red Hill School, Worcester, who have developed the Positive Playtime programme and allowed me to test games out with their children.

A special thank you goes to George Robinson, my editor and 'Teach to Inspire' founder who has supported and encouraged me in the writing of this book. You truly practice what you preach with regards to emotional literacy and leadership and it is an enormous pleasure working with such a generous and kind-hearted person.

Thanks to Barbara Maines, with your eye for detail and getting some of the nitty gritty sorted with regards to the cover and title of the book, and to Mel for your editing and Jess your design.

Finally a big thank you to Amber, Geoff and my mum who have supported me through the writing of two books over a period of 18 months. That's no mean feat and your love and contribution are enormously valued. Thank you.

Foreword

Games can sort out problems, the kind of problems found in interpersonal relationships. They can help social inadequacy by developing cooperation within groups, develop sensitivity to the problems of others through games needing trust, and provide inter-dependency as well as an independence of personal identity.

(Brandes & Howard 1995)

Over my years of working in schools as both a teacher and education consultant, I have heard a common cry from teachers and lunchtime supervisors, 'Help, what can we do about wet play?' It seems that every educator across the country dreads the sound of rain pouring down outside!

You see we know there isn't enough space and that often there is little for children to do which in turn leads to bored and disruptive behaviour. Teachers also dread it because they know that when children have been cooped up indoors all day with little chance to burn off any energy, afternoon lessons often don't go as well, due to wilder and less attentive children!

Playtime is the topic that most frequently raises its head when we get into discussions about managing behaviour and this time in the day can be made or broken according to the playtime programme in place.

In my book 101 Playtime Games (Hoyle, 2008) I laid out the fundamental ideas for running successful playtimes and this book seeks to build on those ideas, specifically looking at wet playtimes and lunchtimes.

My purpose in writing the book is to create a wealth of ideas and outline some simple steps that schools, organisations and parents/carers can take to create a happy, calm, fun, stimulating and socially enjoyable wet playtime.

Introduction

The Value of Playing Together

> Play will be to the 21st century what work was to the last three hundred years of industrial society – our dominant way of knowing, doing and creating value.

> (Pat Kane 2005)

I remember many years ago running Circle Time at an inner city London school and one very articulate seven year old expressing that she didn't like the fact that she had so many clubs after school. She said, 'I don't like it when I have to go to drama, French, piano, netball and gymnastics after school.'

More recently my daughter Amber has been preparing for Key Stage Two SAT's tests. Her primary school tries so hard to not place pressure on the Year Six children. However, governmental target's and children's own will to do well creates stress in their young lives and yet, ironically, psychologists tell us that children under stress don't perform as well or play as well.

The aim of parents/carers, schools and the government is to do the very best for children and sadly with wanting the best they often get caught up with placing greater and greater pressures and demands on them. What then gets lost is a child's freedom to play with unstructured timetables and space of their own.

In my book 101 Playground Games (Hoyle 2008), I wrote about the changes in society and the, '…worrying trend that has appeared with schools shortening or disbanding play altogether.' This also appears evident in children's homes as well.

The Scientific American Mind (2009) says that:

> According to a paper published in 2005 in the Archives of Pediatrics and Adolescent Medicine, children's free-play time dropped by a quarter between 1981 and 1997. Concerned about getting their kids into the right colleges, parents are sacrificing playtime for more structured activities. As early as preschool, youngsters' after-school hours are now being filled with music lessons and sports reducing time for the type of imaginative and rambunctious cavorting that fosters creativity and cooperation.

Blatchford and Baines (2008, 2006) research into the, '…social and educational significance of school break times,' highlights the worrying trend further. Their research showed that school break times are being reduced in time and number across the country and particularly at secondary level. The research showed that break times are overwhelmingly popular with pupils. However, they expressed that, '…they did not get enough time to play, exercise and socialise,' (2008). The research did show that secondary school students in particular wanted longer lunchtimes – many are now only half an hour long. Staff were seen to value break times as a space where pupils got physical exercise and developed important social skills.

Taking away outdoor space and controlling every aspect of the student's environment flies in the face of other government initiatives such as Every Child Matters, Learning Outside the Classroom, Social and Emotional Aspects of Learning (SEAL) and worries about obesity.

Further substantiating these findings is an article in the New York Times (2008) by Robin Marantz Henig highlighting the concerns of parents, educators, psychologists and public health officials:

> Educators fret that school officials are hacking away at recess to make room for an increasingly crammed curriculum. Psychologists complain that overscheduled kids have no time left for the real business of childhood: idle, creative, unstructured free play. Public health officials link insufficient playtime to a rise in childhood obesity. Parents bemoan the fact that kids don't play the way they themselves did – or think they did. And everyone seems to worry that without the chance to play stickball or hopscotch out on the street, to play with dolls on the kitchen floor or climb trees in the woods, today's children are missing out on something essential.

This article is about a 'sold out' talk given by Stuart Brown, president of the National Institute of Play, at New York's public library. Brown created the institute in 1996, after more than 20 years of psychiatric practice and research persuaded him of the dangerous long-term consequences of play deprivation. In his talk he discussed the biological and spiritual underpinnings of play. Brown called play part of the:

> '…developmental sequencing of becoming a human primate. If you look at what produces learning and memory and wellbeing, play is as fundamental as any other aspect of life, including sleep and dreams.'

Increasing Joy and Happiness through Play

I recently visited my daughter's school on a wet play day. What struck me most was the joy-felt giggles and laughter that came from classrooms as children played.

Every Child Matters (DfES 2004) suggests that children learn through fun. Holden (1993) also states that it is through laughter that children relieve stress.

If we are to have happy children in school we need to consider the implication of positive playtimes, whether it be a wet or dry playtime. It is increasingly understood that play has a significant contribution to children's wellbeing, in terms of their mental, emotional, physical and spiritual wellbeing. For many children playtime is the time in their day when they can let go of worries and concerns and engage in fun activities.

Many researchers see play today as a way of developing happiness. McGonigal (2007) quotes Stephen Peterson, University of Michigan, 'We know what makes people happy. It is:

- to have good relationships with other human beings
- to do work you like
- to be a contributing member of some community.'

When children play they develop and build good relationships, do work they love and contribute to the school community.

Play produces the capacity for joy, fun and laughter. Goleman (2007) suggests, '…exactly why playing is so much fun has become clearer with the discovery that the brain circuitry that primes play arouses joy.' The scientist Jaak Pansepp (1993) also explores playfulness, which he sees as the brain's source of joy.

According to neuro science every feeling that we have is a 'neuro chemical event' (Mac Conville, 2009). Danger, stress and anxiety trigger the release of adrenalin and cortisol, which often leads to the freeze, fight or flight response. Positive emotions, which come from positive play and positive social interaction, lead to a cocktail of good chemicals such as, opioids and oxytocin, which make us feel calm, content, secure and safe; dopamine which is the 'motivation chemical' and serotonin the wellbeing, feel good chemical, '…which is a major factor in social and emotional intelligence,' (Sunderland 2006).

Endorphins are the body's natural opiates. They control pain and create pleasure. They are released every time you laugh, relax and exercise. They also create more bonding in the brain so they can make you more intelligent. So when you choose to be happy you also become more intelligent.

The Role of Play in Developing Smart, Socially and Emotionally Intelligent Young People

> At best, IQ contributes about twenty percent to the factors that determine life success, which leaves eighty percent to other forces: forces grouped as emotional intelligence.

> (Goleman 1995)

As we see, play can lead to an increase in positive emotions which in turn can affect emotional intelligence, social intelligence and intelligence.

Sunderland (2006) states, 'The benefits of creative play are many. Research with both humans and other mammals demonstrates that play can lower stress chemicals, enabling us to deal better with stressful situations.'

Research also hints that play actually appears to make chidren smarter. Sunderland (2006) quotes a fascinating study. Rats were given an enriched environment with, '…climbing tubes, novel food and lots of social interaction.' Two months later, the rats had an extra 50,000 brain cells in each side of the hippocampus (one of the key memory centres of the brain).

The Scientific American Mind (Jan 28, 2009) asks, 'But why might play help kids excel?' It comments that, '…animal researchers believe that play serves as a kind of training for the unexpected.' 'Play is like a kaleidoscope,' says evolutionary biologist Marc Bekoff of the University of Colorado at Boulder, in that it is random and creative. The bottom line, he posits, is that play encourages flexibility and creativity that may, in the future, be advantageous in unexpected situations or new environments. Some child psychologists, such as Tufts University child development expert David Elkind, agree. Play is, '…a way in which children learn,' Elkind says, '…and in the absence of play, children miss learning experiences.'

The journal points out that, 'Childhood play is crucial for social, emotional and cognitive development … It makes us better adjusted, smarter and less stressed.' It highlights that, '…kids and animals that do not play when they are young may grow into anxious, socially maladjusted adults.' The journal also comments that Brown, '…has interviewed some 6,000 people about their childhoods and his data suggests that a lack of opportunities for unstructured, imaginative play can keep children from growing into happy, well-adjusted adults. "Free play", as scientists call it, is critical for becoming socially adept, coping with stress and building cognitive skills such as problem-solving.'

The article goes on to suggest that, '…a handful of studies support Brown's conviction that a play-deprived childhood disrupts normal social, emotional and cognitive development in humans and animals.' He and other psychologists worry that limiting free play in kids may result in a generation of anxious, unhappy and socially maladjusted adults. 'The consequence of a life that is seriously play-deprived is serious stuff,' Brown says. 'But it is never too late to start: play also promotes the continued mental and physical wellbeing of adults.'

The article highlights some comments from Pellegrini that, 'Play appears to help us develop strong social skills … You don't become socially competent via teachers telling you how to behave. You learn those skills by interacting with your peers, learning what's acceptable, what's not acceptable.' Children learn to be fair and take turns. They cannot always demand to be the fairy queen or soon they have no playmates. 'They want this thing to keep going, so they're willing to go the extra mile to accommodate others' desires,' he explains. Because kids enjoy the activity, they do not give up as easily in the face of frustration as they might on, say, a math problem which helps them to develop persistence and negotiating abilities.

Keeping things friendly requires a fair bit of communication, arguably the most valuable social skill of all. Play that transpires with peers is the most important in this regard. Studies show that children use more sophisticated language when playing with other children than when playing with adults.

Daniel Goleman (2007) says:

> Playful fun has serious benefits: through years of hard play, children acquire a range of social expertise. For one they learn social savvy, like how to negotiate power struggles, how to cooperate and form alliances, and how to concede with grace … Play offers children a secure space to try out something new in their repertoire with minimum anxiety.

Goleman's (1995) earlier work on emotional intelligence is seen by some to have influenced the development of the governments DfES 2004 Every Child Matters document. This emphasises the fact that emotional wellbeing and pupil performance go hand in hand. In Every Child Matters the five outcomes for children and young people are outlined as follows:

1. Being healthy.
2. Staying safe.
3. Enjoying and achieving.
4. Making a positive contribution.
5. Economic wellbeing.

The continuing influence of Goleman's work is also reflected in the SEAL (June 2005) primary national strategies publications, which seeks to develop and promote the core concepts of the following:

- Self-awareness.
- Managing feelings.
- Self-motivation.
- Empathy.
- Social skills.

Most of the outcomes and concepts from Every Child Matters and SEAL can be supported through creating a whole-school climate of positive play and playtimes, and through many of the games and activities in this book.

As we can see, not only do children enjoy playing and playtimes, they also learn a great deal through games and activities. Playtimes and lunchtimes, then, are not simply an excuse for children to run around and let off steam. In many ways they are also part of the educational and social development of the child, an extension of the classroom.

The Benefits of Organising a Wet Playtimes and Lunchtimes Programme and of Using this Book

Picture this, you are a busy classroom teacher, it's almost lunchtime on a Tuesday and it has started to pour with torrential rain. If your school has a wet playtime policy then everyone in the school will be clear about the procedures, your wet play box will be organised and children will have a stimulating, rewarding playtime experience. However, if you are like a lot of schools across the country you will be scrambling around trying to find activities to entertain the children or you will have just discovered your wet play box needs replenishing!

The problem with wet playtimes is that they happen haphazardly, we never know when they are going to occur and often we are completely unprepared. The aim of this book is to make sure you are prepared and that you have a wealth of ideas up your sleeve.

There are many benefits for children in using this book and running an organised wet playtime programme which may include:

- children playing cooperatively in organised spaces
- happy, entertained children, who are not bored and running around in corridors
- opportunities for socialising and building social skills
- strengthening and development of friendships
- increased emotional wellbeing
- improved cognitive development
- increased resilience
- team work and camaraderie
- fun and joy
- the promotion of children's development, learning, imagination, creativity, independence and interdependence
- stress reduction
- language development
- the development of fine and gross motor skills
- the development of confidence and self-esteem.

In my research to find out more from you about what you wanted included in this book, I travelled across the country talking to teachers, children, lunchtime supervisors, parents and classroom assistants and I discovered that you wanted a book that was inspiring, user friendly, packed with activities, games and ideas that were easy to implement. You also told me that you'd like a book you could just grab off the shelf when it started to rain, that included lots of copiable activities and ideas that supported schools in creating a wet playtime policy that led to happier playtimes. This book is a result of listening to you.

It includes the following:

- Easy to run, stimulating activities and games that can be quickly organised at short notice.

- A selection of copiable resources that can be quickly printed off the CD-ROM or photocopied from the book.

- Ideas to help implement a wet playtime policy.

- Creative ideas to support you in organising wet play.

- Structures for behaviour management at wet playtimes including rewards and encouragers to celebrate children who play well.

- Suggestions for wet play activity boxes and lots of creative ideas for your wet play themed boxes.

So here it is, jam packed with creative ideas, activities, games and activity pages to make those rainy days rainbow filled. Have fun and remember, 'Play is regarded as essential to life long learning, creativity and wellbeing,' Wood (2007).

How to Use this Book

This book and CD-ROM are intended to provide you with a toolkit of ideas that support children, lunchtime supervisors, teachers, classroom assistants, parents, play leaders, after school clubs, youth and church groups and indeed anyone involved in the organisation of a wet playtime. It includes games that are great for letting off steam and activities that encourage creativity, the development of thinking skills, social skills and emotional wellbeing. Many of the activities link into other curriculum areas, such as Circle Time, art and technology, maths, literacy, the thinking curriculum and so on.

I have used some of the thinking games activities myself with gifted and talented pupils and when supply teaching. You can use the circle and parachute games as part of your PHSE and SEAL curriculum. Both of these include games that are ideal for your class Circle Time. You will find that many of the games can be played anywhere from a classroom or school hall to outside when the rain ceases.

So although this is largely a wet playtime book, be flexible and have fun with the activities and please do use this as a cross curricular resource, embracing the opportunity to bring play and learning together.

There are 101 games to choose from (researched and field tested). The games and activities are divided up into two sections which include:

1. Wet Play Activity Boxes

This section focuses on the creation of the three themed activity boxes and is packed with creative ideas and copiable resources to support teachers and lunchtime supervisors in keeping children entertained during wet playtimes.

- Thinking Games.
- Paper Play and Technology Challenges.
- Quiz and Puzzle Activities.

2. Active Games

This section is filled with a selection of active games for playing in the classroom or hall.

- Circle Games.
- Parachute Games.
- Active Games for Letting Off Steam.
- Singing, Rhymes and Dancing Games.

You will find that most of the activities and games can be organised in the classroom whilst the games under the heading Active Games can be played in the hall.

Each game is specifically marked with the age range, ideal number of players required and equipment needed and what to do.

Terminology

Leader – the player who leads and organises the game

Player, child, and student – These terms are inter mingled throughout the book.

Game per Page

Most games are on one page and have the same layout:

- Name of game.
- Age range.
- Ideal number of players.
- Equipment needed.
- What to do.
- Rules.
- Variations.

Rules and Variations

With the rules and variations sections you may find information that I have added however these sections are also intended for you to use. By adding your own rules and variations, we hope that these pages become even more user friendly.

CD-ROM of the Games

This book includes a CD-ROM. It is intended as a resource that will support you in endless ways. I would suggest that you print off sections of the book and put them into the activity boxes. You may want to put some of the games onto coloured card and then laminate them.

You can also log onto other games and activity websites from the CD-ROM.

Gender

Rather than use he/she throughout the book, which can become very cumbersome, I have used both genders equally throughout the range of games. In no way at any point do I want to suggest a stereotype in any particular kind of game. It is intended that you adapt the gender to the children you are working with. He and she is just used throughout as an example.

Organising Wet Playtimes

There are many ways you can organise wet playtimes. This book brings together ideas, resources and stimulating activities that I have tried and tested over the last 12 years in schools. In this section I have included many things to think about when creating a whole-school wet playtime policy from doing Strengths, Weaknesses, Opportunities, Threat's (SWOT) analyses or Positive, Minus and Interesting (PMI's) to organising your rules, rewards and consequences systems. Please feel free to dip in and out of the book and use it in a way that is most useful to you, your school and children.

Firstly let's remember that playtime is a whole-school issue and one that everyone needs to be involved in, not just the lunchtime supervisors.

Initially when looking at your playtimes and wet play days consult with everyone in the school. Get everyone together, lunchtime supervisors, children, teachers, teaching assistants, parents/carers, governors and do a SWOT analysis or PMI (see end of this section). The SWOT is often used in business and leadership and is intended to improve strengths, remove weaknesses, grasp opportunities and reduce threats. The PMI is a graphic organiser and frequently used in the thinking curriculum and inquiry learning. PMI charts were formalised by Edward de Bono in 1992.

So firstly list out all the positives – everything that works well on wet play days. Lunchtime supervisors often have a wealth of experience and insight into this time in the school day, many have worked as supervisors for ten years or more. They will have seen games come and go and are good sources of information and inspiration. For example:

Positives

- Video time.
- Whole classroom activities, like the disco.
- Wet play leaders.
- We haven't had many wet lunchtimes this year!

Celebrate these strengths, they may also be indicators that help inform future wet play planning.

Then make a list of all the minus's that occur on wet play days, this list is usually longer! For example:

Minus's

- Bored disruptive children.
- Lack of stimulating activities.
- Lack of space.
- Noisy.
- Lack of equipment or activities for children to do.
- Children not allowed to use classroom equipment.
- Wet play boxes not up-to-date.
- Children often floating around the school and not in their classroom.
- Hard to monitor with not enough supervisors.

Opportunities

Money available next term from PTA for wet play resources.

Fete in the summer months, possibility to look for resources for wet play boxes.

Threats

Children loitering in the toilets.

Lack of staffing in some classrooms.

Once you have composed these lists, think of solutions and remove or reduce the minus's and threats. Some solutions will be easy to solve, others may need time, funding, resources and so on. Capitalise and improve on your strengths and grasp any opportunities.

Similarly, consult with the children. Start by talking with them about activities that they enjoy doing or would like to do at wet playtime. You may find that they have numerous suggestions. If you adopt the PMI strategy, they will also be able to tell you what currently works and what doesn't. Alternatively some schools organise Circle Times and others do questionnaires, using web survey's such as survey monkey or survey gizmo (see Appendix for website) to get their input.

Children need things to play with at wet playtime and it is important that adequate resources are provided, so make sure that a budget is set each year to provide for establishing and then updating wet play activities. Many local authorities will supply funding for playtimes. So do remember to allocate some of that budget to wet play.

Plan wisely, create short-term, easy to implement plans and build some of your more long-term plans into your school development plan.

Remember that even though it is wet, this is children's playtime and an important time in their day to let off steam, connect with their friends and have some fun. It is also the time in the day where social, emotional and behavioural skills are learnt.

Rules

At wet playtime it is important to have clear and consistent rules in place. Ideally the rules will have been thought through at the beginning of term with the class teacher and children. Children should think about how they can safely move around the school, walking, not running in corridors and so on. I have spoken with many lunchtime supervisors over the years who have told me that children often try to play them off against teachers. For instance, they tell them that they are allowed to go down to another class or get certain classroom equipment out because their teacher has said they could. More often than not their teacher knows nothing about this! It is thus essential that rules and expectations are written down and placed on the wall of the classroom and in the wet play box and any changes to plans, rules and so on are clearly discussed with supervisors. When children know that we are all communicating clearly and working together everyone's life is easier.

Some basic rules that I find work well in all games are:
- Be kind.
- Play fairly.
- Be safe.

Rewards

The reward is always that they get to have fun!

Raffle tickets or 'Star Player', 'Star Child', 'Caught Being Good' tokens (see Resources section), can also be given out. The tokens or raffle tickets are a reward system for individual children. You may choose between any of these rewards or you may choose to use them all! When children are seen playing cooperatively, being kind, being gentle, winning a game and so on they get a paper reward token or raffle ticket. The child at the end of wet play with the most tokens/raffle tickets receives a 'Great Wet Playtime Award' or prize.

The Great Wet Playtime Class Award

Lunchtime supervisors, teachers and play leaders are encouraged to give out raffle tickets/tokens throughout wet play. The class at the end of playtime who has the most receives a special certificate or prize that is given out in the next assembly. Alternatively fruit, healthy snacks or stickers can also be given out. This is an easy to manage system. Lunchtime supervisors just need to make sure that they have a good supply of raffle tickets or tokens.

Consequences

The consequence of breaking rules is that they have a verbal warning. If they then break the rule again, they are out of the game or activity for ten minutes and usually have to sit in a solitary place in the hall or classroom away from other children, thinking through which rule they have broken and which rule they should be keeping, who they need to apologise to and so on. Children can join in the game or activity once they have had time out and/or as long as relationships have been restored.

If the children are organising the games and activities they are generally very clear with one another as to what is acceptable and what's not!

Lunchtime Supervisors

Once schools have decided on the activities they would like to have out at wet play, it is helpful to run a training day or afternoon, introducing and familiarising all staff with ideas from the book.

Lunchtime supervisors frequently have a challenging role at wet playtime and it makes a huge difference when everyone is working together and towards the same goals and aims. Ideally it helps if supervisors can work with the teachers on establishing a wet playtime policy.

Play Coordinator

An adult should hold the post of play coordinator. This person is responsible for ensuring wet playtimes and lunchtimes are properly resourced, this includes creating all the wet play boxes and ensuring that they are regularly replenished.

Rainbow Activity Leader Training

In '101 Playground Games' (Hoyle, 2008) I wrote about how to set up your playground activity leader's (PALS). I would suggest that you use this same group of children as your wet play leaders, since they will already have a range of leadership skills and will be competent in playing games and organising activities. The PALS will need to be informed about wet play procedures and introduced and familiarised with a selection of activities from this book.

Alternatively if you don't have PALS already in place or you would like to select a different group of children to be on wet play duty, then you should organise some additional training. I refer to the wet play group of children as Rainbow Activity Leaders (RALs).

Training the Rainbow Activity Leaders

When considering adopting this system in your school, please give consideration to the following:

- How many RALs do you need, given the size of your school, number of classes and so on?
- What class or which room will they be allocated to?
- What activity can they teach?
- How would the RALs be chosen?
- What support will they need?
- Which pupils will be chosen? Ideally it be Year 5 and 6.

Their Role

To encourage and organise games and activities in the classrooms and hall, during wet play.

Training and Support

Ideally a lunchtime supervisor and a teacher will take responsibility for the RALs, their training and ongoing support.

Step 1 – Discuss roles and responsibilities, rules for themselves, wet play rules, rota's, period of time that they are elected to be a RAL (usually all term), how to set up a classroom, activities, wet play boxes, classroom organisation and so on.

Step 2 – Introduce a selection of games and activities from the book. I suggest that you copy the 'Circle Time Games' section of the book and give each child a pack of games that they can keep and use as a reference. This will give the RALs a selection of games to learn and introduce to the children.

Step 3 – The RALs plan and organise a game to play with a class.

Step 4 – The RALs evaluate how the game went and continue to learn new games.

Step 5 – The RALs choose a uniform that distinguishes them when they are on duty, this may be a rainbow coloured baseball cap, bib, badge and so on.

Step 6 – RALs are given specific responsibilities for wet play days and assigned classes. There are always 2-3 RALs per class. Some may be elected as equipment monitors with their role being to put equipment out.

Step 7 – RALs are taken around the school and introduced to the children and class teachers, they learn where wet play boxes and equipment are kept.

Step 8 – The RALs are introduced in assembly to all the school.

Step 9 – The RALs contribute to 'wet playtime news' at assemblies.

Step 10 – The RALs meet termly with an assigned adults who supports them.

Ongoing Support

The RALs need to have a regular time to talk about their experiences, the successes and the challenges with a specified adult, usually a lunchtime supervisor or a teacher. Ideally this meeting is half termly or termly depending on how much rain has fallen! The RALs should be known to all staff so that they can give support and encouragement. Their parents/carers can also be informed.

At the end of the term and their time as a RAL they receive a certificate to thank them for their contribution and hard work. This is given out in assembly.

There are lots of different ways of organising a wet playtime and you have many choices. I have outlined a few ways that have proved successful in the many schools I have worked in. I hope they provide children and supervisors with a system that is manageable and effective and also leads to fun and harmony – a wet playtime filled with many rainbow ideas!

'We don't stop playing because we grow old; we grow old because we stop playing.'

George Bernard Shaw.

Swot Analysis for Wet Playtimes

Strengths	Weaknesses

Opportunities	Threats

Organizing Wet Playtimes

PMI for Wet Playtimes

Positive	Minus	Interesting
List all the positives, advantages and benefits.	List all the negatives, disadvantages and drawbacks.	What if... I wonder...

WET PLAY ACTIVITY BOXES

Thinking Games

Paper Play and Technology Challenges

Quiz and Puzzle Activities

Organising Wet Play Activity Boxes

A system that has proved very successful in many schools across the country during wet playtime is the Wet Play Activity Box. When adopting this system each class makes up their own activity box. It contains resources, activity pages, games sheets and so on that they don't normally have access to in the school day. The box is regularly replenished and can be changed from term to term. If you are feeling adventurous there are lots of alternative ideas that develop the single box theme, which are included in the next few pages.

Preparation

Ask friends, parents/carers and staff to help collect and prepare the boxes.

Consider where these boxes can be stored.

This box is only allowed out at wet play, so that it remains a special treat.

Decide who will help to clear up and sort the contents in each box at the end of wet breaks.

School newsletter – make a request to parents/carers for resources that may be used for wet play boxes and activities. This may include toys and activities/games that they no longer use. I always make a point of saying that all games and jigsaws and so on need to have all their pieces, so please only donate if they are fully functional!

Here are some request suggestions that you can make to parents and carers.

Our school needs:

- Jigsaws.
- Games.
- DVD's.
- Music CD's.
- Books.
- Puzzles.
- Construction kits – lego, mobilo and so on.
- Dressing-up clothes.
- Knitting needles and wool.
- Colouring in pictures, dot to dots and so on.
- Scrap paper, coloured card, tissue paper.
- Comics/magazines.
- Boxes/recycled materials for creative activities/box modelling.
- Imaginative play (small worlds).

Every class will need plastic cubes or boxes to store the resources in. I would suggest that in each box contains a selection of age appropriate activities which may include some of the following:

- Pack of cards.
- 2-3 music and story CD's .
- A selection of DVD's.
- A selection of board games, snakes and ladders, ludo, draughts, chess, dominoes.
- Jigsaws.
- Knitting.
- Mazes.
- Plasticine or playdough.
- Construction kits – lego and so on.
- Crayons, pencils, paper.
- Paint and brushes.
- Dressing-up clothes.
- Imaginative play (small worlds).
- Books and comics.
- Boxes/recycled materials for creative activities/box modelling and so on.

You have a few options once you have this box in place.

Option 1 – Classroom General Activity Box

Three or four wet play activities from the box can be laid out in different parts of the classroom, creating different activity zones. For example, quiet zone, games zone, creative zone, imaginary play zone, construction zone, DVD zone, disco zone, meditation zone, painting and drawing zone, listening to music or stories zone, paper play and technology zone, thinking games zone, reading zone, circle games zone, quiz and puzzle zone and so on.

Option 2 – Wet Play Activity Box Themes – Themed Boxes for Rainy Days

These boxes have particular themes as opposed to a selection of different activities for children to do, such as:

- Thinking Games.
- Paper Play and Technology Challenges.
- Quiz and Puzzle Activities.

All the above themes are in section one of this book. Each section provides a wealth of ideas to keep children entertained.

Some classes like to have a general activity box and a themed box.

Organising the Themed Boxes

- Use a plastic cube/container to store all the materials needed for your theme.
- Each theme needs to be age appropriate.
- When using activities and games from the book for your themed box, firstly print out the activities you want to use from the CD-ROM onto coloured card, laminate them so that they will last and then gather all the equipment suggested and store it inside the box.
- Practise playing some of the games and have a go at some of the activities, so you feel prepared when the next wet lunchtime strikes.
- Print out a selection of the copiable resources and worksheets

Other Wet Play Activity Box Ideas

There are hundred's of ideas you could use to create additional themed boxes. Below are a few suggestions. Please do use your own creative ideas and make sure you get the children actively involved in the planning stage too.

Pirates

The pirate theme is always popular with young children. When making up a pirate theme box you may like to use a selection of ideas from below:

- Children can make their own eye patches using card, wool/elastic.
- Have a selection of books on pirates.
- Sticky labels are great for making pirate name badges.
- Make sure you have some thick tights or socks for storing 'pieces of eight'.
- Card tubes make great telescopes, so get parents to donate these from home.
- Have paper and pencils ready for making treasure maps, drawing skull and crossbones.
- See if you can get hold of pirate puzzles, colouring pictures, materials to make flags.

Other Themed Ideas

Wool activities – for finger knitting, plaiting, making pom poms and so on.

Badge making – using sticky labels, get children to decorate them and then they can wear them.

Feelings – Gather a collection of objects, for example, Sponges, comb, toothbrush, spoon, rubber, piece of lego and so on and a blindfold. Get the players put on the blindfold and then feel an object from the bag and then and guess what it is.

Making collages/montages and mosaics.

Games – make up a box with a selection of board games and so on.

Create your own ideas for activity boxes.

Option 3 – Whole-Class Activities in their Classroom.

This can include a selection of games from either section where the whole class can be involved in the same activity.

Option 4 – Whole-School Activity Zones

Different zones can be created throughout the school, so that children can freely wander and find an activity they are interested in. This is probably easier to organise at the lunch break. The zones may be the classrooms, hall, library and so on.

Suggestions for activity zones:

- Reading zone – library.
- Video/DVD in the hall.
- Parachute games in the hall.
- Circle Time or singing and dancing games in the hall.
- Active games for letting off steam in the hall.
- Paper play and technology challenges.
- Singing and dancing games.
- Disco and dancing.
- Quiz and puzzle activities.
- Quiet games zone.
- Umbrella zone– children can borrow an umbrella and go for a walk in the rain.

Children have two choices with this system:

1. They can choose one activity for the whole lunchtime.

2. They can choose to wander around the school and try different activities. The latter involves more careful consideration since of course there could be a danger in children wandering around the school and getting themselves into trouble. To avoid this I would suggest you discuss the school rules, their responsibilities and any additional rules needed inside the school during a wet lunchtime. For example, walk in the corridors, move quickly from one activity to another.

You can always trial this system and see if it works. It's certainly worth giving children the opportunity and if they want to make it work then they can make it a success.

At the end of a wet lunchtime make sure that staff and children tidy up 5-10 minutes prior to the bell going and then ensure that they all return to class promptly.

Wet Play Activity Box Themes

1. Thinking Games.
2. Paper Play and Technology Challenges.
3. Quiz and Puzzle Activities.

This focuses on the creation of the three themed activity boxes and is packed with creative ideas and copiable resources to support teachers and lunchtime supervisors in keeping children entertained during wet playtimes.

When selecting activities for these wet play boxes:

- choose age appropriate activities for your class/children

- print and laminate the activity pages

- make sure you have a supply of the copiable sheets, grids, templates, colouring in's and so on and that these are regularly replenished

- ensure that you have all the resources and equipment the children will need.

THINKING GAMES

Thinking Games

For this wet play activity box you will need to stock up regularly on the resources and activity pages.

Resource Box

Marshmallows.

Toothpicks/cocktail sausage sticks.

Old tin cans with labels removed.

Metre rule.

Pack of playing cards.

Paper/Squared paper.

Pens and pencils.

Pack of cards.

Card – thin and thick.

Newspapers.

Tray.

Timer/clock.

Dice.

There are a wide variety of games and activities in this section to use in your wet play themed activity box which encourage the development of children's thinking skills.

Whilst researching some of the games for this section I discovered some interesting facts that I thought you may find informative.

'Kim's Game' is a game that is often played by boy scouts, girl guides and other children's groups. The game develops a person's capacity to observe and remember details. The name is derived from Rudyard Kipling's 1901 novel Kim in which the hero, Kim, plays the game during his training as a spy. It is great for developing memory and observation skills.

Noughts and Crosses, or Tic Tac Toe as it is known in America, is probably the most common pencil and paper game around in the western world. The rules are extremely simple. I remember playing it as a child drawing noughts and crosses with a twig in the sand. Surprisingly, some game manufacturers succeed in selling this as a board game. The games origins lie in ancient Egypt where the nine square grid or 'magic square 'was filled with numbers that were believed to contain mystical powers.

Hangman is an excellent way of building vocabulary, concentration, memory and improving spelling skills. This well loved game was the inspiration for the TV programme Wheel of Fortune, in which players also seek to uncover a mystery word, letter by letter.

The hangman diagram is designed to look like a hanging man. Although debates have arisen about the questionable taste of this picture, it is still a very popular game with children and families today. A common alternative for teachers of young learners is to draw an apple tree with ten apples, erasing or crossing out the apples as the guesses are used up.

The exact nature of the diagram differs from person to person. Some players draw the gallows before play and draw parts of the man's body (traditionally the head, then the torso, then the left arm, then the right arm, then the left leg, then the right leg). Some players begin with no diagram at all drawing the individual elements of the gallows as part of the game, effectively giving the guessing players more chances.

'The origins of Hangman are obscure, but it seems to have arisen in Victorian times,' says Augarde (2003).

The game is mentioned in Alice Bertha Gomme's Traditional Games in 1894 under the name 'Birds, Beasts and Fishes'. The rules are simple, a player writes down the first and last letters of a word for an animal and the other player guesses the letters in between.

In other sources the game is called 'Gallows', 'The Game of Hangin'', or 'Hanger'.

Battleships – the paper grid game predates the First World War. Nowadays you can get handheld battleship games, some of which have sound effects!

Beetle – this game was also once known as Bugs and when I was young you could buy the game and create a plastic beetle! This game was first marketed by Schaper Toys in 1948 as Cootie. Players rolled a die and pieced together a plastic flea, according to the numbers rolled, from parts supplied in a box. It is now just as easily played with a pencil and paper. You may be able to buy or find special dice that have the six faces marked with letters corresponding to the beetle body parts – B-ody, H-ead, L-eg, E-yes, A-ntenna and T-ail or you could make one yourself.

There are a vast variety of games here to keep you and the children thinking. Some games are brief and can be played in a short amount of time, such as Card Building, Boxes, Hangman, I Spy, Beetle and Noughts and Crosses. Other games such as Marshmallow Towers and the Green Baked Bean Challenge, We're Going on a Picnic, Charades and Kim's Game may take up most of a lunchbreak.

Some good websites for Thinking Games are listed in the Apendix.

1. Marshmallow Towers

Age Range: 6-11
Ideal Number of Players: Teams of 3 or 4
Equipment Needed: 100 toothpicks, two cups of small marshmallows, a ruler or metre stick

What to Do

Using only the materials provided, build the tallest free-standing tower you can.
Spend five minutes brainstorming ideas for structuring the tower. After the five minutes, discussion time is over and the students can start constructing their tower.
Students have ten minutes to complete it.
Use a metre rule or ruler to measure the height of each tower.
Discuss the strengths of each tower.
For fun, allow students to test the sturdiness of their towers by trying to blow them down.

Reflections:
- How did working in teams make this activity easier to accomplish than working alone?
- How did working in a team make this activity harder to accomplish than working alone?
- What is the advantage of working in a team?
- What is the disadvantage of working in a team?

Rules
Use only the materials you have been given and ask if you want to use the other teams resources.

Variations
You could use newspapers to make the tallest tower. Players would need to roll up newspaper and stick it together with sellotape or masking tape.
Another idea would be to make a bridge with lolly sticks and masking tape.

2. The Blue Baked Bean Challenge

Age Range: 7-11
Ideal Number of Players: 20+ divided into teams
Equipment Needed: A food tin with the label removed

What to Do

A disaster has occurred at the local baked bean factory. Somehow harmless blue dye has found its way into hundred's of tins of baked beans. The baked bean factory is now facing bankruptcy if they are unable to sell these tins of beans.

You are an expert in advertising and marketing and have created successful advertisements in the past for lots of products that nobody really wants or needs. Since you know that the blue dye is harmless you want to help this company out and they have offered to pay you lots of money if you can enable them to sell these baked beans.

Your challenge is to create an advertisement suitable for television that will convince consumers to buy the blue baked beans.

Select a panel of judges, usually one or two players. You have 30 minutes to prepare your advertisement. A warning will be given after 20 minutes and you will then have one minute to perform the advertisement to the judges.

You will be scored as follows:

Teamwork during preparation and performance = 20 points.
Creativity = 20 points.
Entertainment value = 10 points.

The judges then say: 'Your time starts now.'

Rules

Stay with your own team, no copying or poaching ideas.

Variations

Instead of baked beans you could use any other tinned food.

3. Pelmanism

Age Range: 5-11
Ideal Number of Players: Any
Equipment Needed: One pack of playing cards

What to Do

This is a good game to train memory and observation. The aim of the game is to collect as many pairs as is possible.

Lay the cards face down on the table. One player is chosen who starts by turning two cards over and showing the other players what they are. If they are a pair, such as 3's or 8's or kings, she picks them up, but if they are two different cards she must lay them face down again in exactly the same place.

The other players must note the cards and try to remember them.

The next player on the left then turns up two cards. If one of these is the same as a card turned up by the first player, he may take the pair, provided he can remember where the original card was, and then have another turn. If he turns up a different card by mistake, he must replace it.

The game continues until all the cards are matched. The winner is the player with the most pairs.

Variations:

If you have not played this game before, try using only twelve or eighteen cards at first, making sure you choose six or nine pairs, until you become used to remembering them. As you improve, you can add more cards.

With younger children, you could use snap cards or cards with pictures on them.

4. Battleships

Age Range: 7-11
Ideal Number of Players: 2
Equipment Needed: You will need squared paper, 10 squares by 10 squares, or the Battleship Grid

What to Do

Number the squares A-J and 1 to 10 or use grid provided on page 51.
Each player has one copy of the Battleship Grid which represents the ocean. Without allowing his opponent to see, he positions his fleet of battleships. Firstly he marks out one battleship (four consecutive horizontal or vertical squares), two cruisers (three consecutive horizontal or vertical squares), three destroyers (two adjacent squares each) and four submarines (one square each). The squares representing each ship in the fleet are outlined and shaded in. Ships may not be positioned on the diagonal.

Now battle commences!

The aim of the game is to sink your opponents fleet through a series of 'hits'. Players sit so that they cannot see each others papers during play.
One player starts the game by first 'firing' his 'shot', saying, for example, 'I am aiming at A2, G9 and J10,' naming three squares that he thinks might be occupied by his opponents fleet. Then he marks them down on his spare piece of paper so that he does not aim at those numbers again.
The other player has to tell him whether he has made a 'hit' and crosses off the appropriate square or squares, though he needs not tell his opponent which of his ships has been damaged. Then the other player fires his first 'shot' in a similar fashion and so on. A ship is considered sunk when each square has been hit by the other player. The winner is the first to sink his opponent's whole fleet.

Rules

There must be at least one empty square between ships and once they are positioned they cannot be moved.

Variations

You could use a treasure map idea as an alternative idea. Instead of having ships you could have pieces of treasure and the winner would be the person who discovered the most treasure.

5. Kim's Game

Age Range: 5-11
Ideal Number of Players: 10+
Equipment Needed: A tray, paper, pens, a selection of objects, 1 minute timer

What to Do

A play leader collects a number of articles and places them on a tray, for example, knives, spoons, pencil, pen, stones, book. No more than about ten to start with, increasing the objects after each completed game.

The play leader covers them all with a cloth and asks the others to sit round, where they can see the tray, and uncovers it for one minute. Then each of them must write a list of all the articles that they canj remember.

The one who remembers the most wins the game.

Rules

No peeking under the cloth. Do not copy what others are writing.

6. Card Building

Age Range: 5-11
Ideal Number Of Players: 2+
Equipment Needed: A pack of cards, a firm surface – preferably non-slip

What to Do

This game requires patience. You can play it on a firm surface or carpeted area. Just make sure there are no draughts.

Start with a basic formation which can be enlarged upwards and outwards. Balance cards as shown in. You can make several of these buildings close together and join them by laying cards along the side. Build another layer on top in the same way and another on top of that.

7. Flower Fun

Age Range: 5-7
Ideal Number of Players: 1
Equipment Needed: Coloured pens or pencils, The Flower Fun activity page

What to Do

Use the key to colour the flower.

4   =   red
5   =   yellow
6   =   green
7   =   orange
8   =   brown

There is a large version of the illustration on page 52.

8. Boxes

Age Range: 7-11
Ideal Number Of Players: 2
Equipment Needed: Pencil or pen for each player, paper or the Boxes Games Square Grid

What to Do

This simple little game can be played almost anywhere at anytime and it's addictive! Opponents compete to make the greatest number of boxes out of a dot grid. As players catch on to the strategy, they can vary the game to make it more challenging.

To begin, players draw a square grid of 16 dots with four even rows of four dots. More experienced players may prefer to use the 100 dot grid resource on page 53.

Players now take turns drawing lines connecting any two dots that are next to each other. The lines must be either horizontal or vertical (no diagonals) and each player may draw only one line per turn at the outset. As the lines accumulate, each player tries to be the one who can close up a four dot box by drawing the fourth line. When a player completes a box, she claims that box with her initial and then draws another line (see diagram) and she can keep going again as long as she keeps completing boxes.

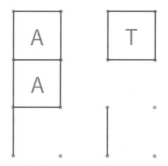

Sometimes, drawing the fourth line on one box can start a chain reaction. That fourth line might be the third line on another box, to which the player can then add a fourth line, which might again be a third line on yet another box and so on. When that player can't complete any more boxes, it's finally the other players turn again.

The game is over when all the dots are connected and all the boxes are filled in. The player with the most boxes is the winner.

Variations

In a variation of the game, players try to complete the smallest, rather than the greatest, number of boxes. In this case, the player who has the fewest boxes at the end of the game is the winner.

9. Hangman

Age Range: 6-11
Ideal Number of Players: 2+
Equipment Needed: Pencil and paper or whiteboard and markers

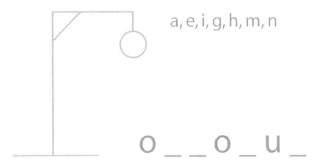

a, e, i, g, h, m, n

o _ _ o _ u _

What to Do

To start with, one player thinks of a word and on a piece of paper draws a line of dashes to represent the letters of the word. If, for example, the player thinks of the word 'octopus' then he needs to draw seven dashes. The opponents then try to work out what the word is.

To do this players take turns guessing which letters make up the word. Whenever someone guesses correctly the letter is written in the appropriate blank or blanks if the letter appears more than once in a word (like o in 'octopus').

At any time as the letters get filled in, a player may use her turn to guess the whole word. A savvy strategy when playing this game is to guess the vowels first, since almost every word has at least one.

Danger occurs when a player guesses a letter that is not in that word. In that case the invalid letter is written down at the top of the page in a discarded letter area. Then the hangman picture starts with the base pole of the gallows being drawn. As the players continue to think of letters and get them wrong, increasing parts of the hangman get added to the picture. Next is top of gallows (thus creating an upside down L), then the stick figure gets created starting with the head, then body, first leg, second leg, first arm, second arm, eyes, nose, mouth and so on.

Players keep calling out letters in turn until the word or the hangman is complete.

The player who completes the word before the hangman is drawn is the winner.

The drawer wins if the hangman is completed before the word is guessed.

Variations

Hangman is a traditional game, though some may see the idea of having a hanging man somewhat distasteful. An alternative that is frequently used by teachers of young children is to draw an apple tree with ten apples, erasing or crossing out the apples as the guesses are used up.

10. I Spy

Age Range: 4-11
Ideal Number of Players: 3+
Equipment Needed: None

What to Do

Thousands of children around the world enjoy 'I Spy'. The game is loads of fun because there are few rules and you can play it almost anywhere. It is also an educational game for younger children who are starting to identify objects by colours and initial letters. My family tend to play it in the car on car journeys and it has always been a great wet weather game.

One player silently selects an object that can be seen by all the players.

This player says, 'I spy with my little eye, something that is...' and then gives some description of the object, such as 'something that is red', 'something that is square' or 'something that is small'.

The other players take turns trying to guess what the object is.

Let the player who correctly guesses the selected item pick the next object or have all players take turns in a set order. This may be best if you are playing with younger children who may not be so good at guessing.

Offer extra clues if the players are completely stumped.

Variations

Alphabet I Spy – in this version of I Spy, suited for slightly older children (7-11) the clue is the first letter of the object's name rather than its colour, shape and so on. For example, if the object was a whiteboard, the player would say, 'I spy with my little eye something beginning with w.'

11. Beetle

Age Range: 6-11
Ideal Number of Players: 2-6
Equipment Needed: Table or other flat surface, one dice, pencil and paper for each player

What to Do

This is a simple and yet exciting game that can be played by children who don't even like creepy crawlies. It's also a great way of introducing children to using a die and die skills!
Each player starts with a blank piece of paper. The aim is to draw a beetle over the course of the game. This is dependent on your die throws.
Players sit around a table or even on the floor.
Players throw the die and the one who scores the highest goes first. If any players roll the same number they roll again until the tie is broken.
The first player opens the game by rolling the die.
If a one is thrown the player may start by drawing a round beetle body. However, if she throws any other number she cannot go and the die passes to the next player on the left where he too tries to roll a one. Each player gets one roll per turn.
To complete the beetle the numbers must be rolled in order from 1 to 6.
The body parts correspond with the number rolled.
1 = body.   2 = head.   3 = a leg.   4 = an eye.   5 = an antenna.
6 = the tail.

Play continues with players aiming for all the other body parts. The beetle must have a body, a head, two antennae, two eyes, six legs and a tail. The player who finishes drawing the beetle first, wins the game.

Variations

Use two dice to speed up play or even develop a more complex beetle to draw.
Another version is played in which players score a point for each part of the beetle they draw. A series of games are played and the player who reaches an agreed total first (say 50 points) wins.

12. Noughts and Crosses

Age Range: 4-11
Ideal Number of Players: 2
Equipment Needed: Pencil and paper

What to Do

The aim of the game it to get three of your own symbols, noughts or crosses, in a row either horizontally, vertically or diagonally.
To start, one player draws two vertical lines crossed with two horizontal lines thus creating a grid of nine squares.

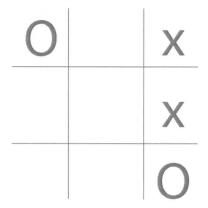

One player uses the symbol 'X' the other 'O'.
Players decide who will go first. Taking turns, the players alternately put an 'X' or 'O' in a empty space in the grid. The first player to fill a row with three of their symbol is the winner.
If neither player is able to complete a line of three symbols the game is considered a draw.

Rules

Players should be encouraged to play as offensively as is possible. Any players who makes marks in the three corners or in the centre square and two corners are almost guaranteed to win.

Variations

An alternative ending which is used in some countries is that the first player to get three in a row draws a line through her symbols and then needs to call out 'noughts and crosses' or 'tic, tac, toe' to win the game.

13. We are Going on a Picnic

Age Range: 5-11
Ideal Number of Players: 10+
Equipment Needed: Lots on inner smiles

What to Do

In this game only the leader needs to know the full set of rules. This is a lateral thinking and trick game.

The leader starts the game and asks the other players to join in and try to guess what the rules of the game are. She also points out that it's a bit of a mind trick game.

The game starts with, 'Hi, I'm Therese and I'm going on a picnic and I'm taking some tea bags, who wants to come?'

Players start guessing.

'Hi, I'm Dominic. Yes I'd like to come and bring a pillow.' Therese responds, 'No, Dominic, you can't come...'

Finally Ayesha gets it and says, 'Hi, I'm Ayesha and I'd like to come and bring some apples.' The trick when playing the game is to know that what you are to bring has to start with the first letter of your name. So Dominic would say, 'Can I bring my dogs?' and Therese would say, 'Yes Dominic you can bring your dogs.'

Players who haven't worked out the trick often get very irate and frustrated. The game ends with the leader explaining what the trick/rule was to those who didn't manage to guess how to play!

Make sure that only one person knows the rules and only one person gets to read this games page!

14. Charades

Age Range: 8+
Ideal Number of Players: 6+
Equipment Needed: None

What to Do

Charades is an acting and guessing game. Players act out a word or phrase. Charades can be played with any type of word or phrase; but with children, you may find that movie titles work best. Most children are familiar with many simple movie titles. And even the youngest can do Pinocchio! There are many variations of how to play Charades. This is just one format.

Players write words or phrases that fall into any of several categories, for example, books, films, TV programme, song onto pieces of scrap paper. Players make sure that they also write their name at the bottom of the scrap paper. The papers are then folded in half and mixed up in a bowl or hat. To begin with one player picks a charade out of the hat. She announces the name at the bottom of the paper and that player sits out the game. When acting out the charade, for starters indicate to your team whether you're going to mime the title of a movie, book, song or TV programme.

Here is a guide to some of the standard gestures:

- Movie: pretend to crank an old-fashioned movie camera.

- Book: pretend to be reading.

- TV programme: draw a square in the air for a TV screen.

- Song: Pretend to sing (silently).

- To divide the word into syllables: lay down x number of fingers on your forearm (where x is the number of syllables). To act out the first syllable, lay down one finger on your arm and so on.

- Little word: bring your thumb and index fingers close together. The people guessing should now call out every little word they can think of ('on, in, the, and') until you gesticulate wildly to indicate the right word.

- Longer version of the word: pretend to stretch an elastic.

- Shorter version of the word: chop with your hand.

- Close, keep guessing: frantically wave hands to keep the guesses coming.

- Whole phrase at once: sweep your arms in a big circle to indicate 'whole thing'.

- Past tense: wave your hand downwards behind your back.

- Sounds like: cup your hand around your ear.

14. Charades (Continued)

The player acts out the word or phrase and the others have to guess what it is. When the word or phrase is finally guessed, another actor takes his turn.

Rules

Talking or mouthing is strictly forbidden. The game can get pretty loud and raucous, but that is part of the fun!

15. How Many Shapes?

Age Range: 4-6
Ideal Number Of Players: 1
Equipment Needed: Coloured pens or pencils, the How Many Shapes?
activity page

What to Do

Look at the pictures and count the correct number of shapes.

There is a large version of the illustration on page 54.

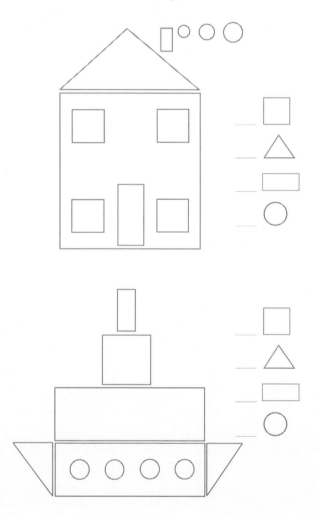

Variations

The shapes can be coloured in.

Battleships Grid

My Ships

	A	B	C	D	E	F	G	H	I	J
1										
2										
3										
4										
5										
6										
7										
8										
9										
10										

Enemy Hits

	A	B	C	D	E	F	G	H	I	J
1										
2										
3										
4										
5										
6										
7										
8										
9										
10										

Thinking Games

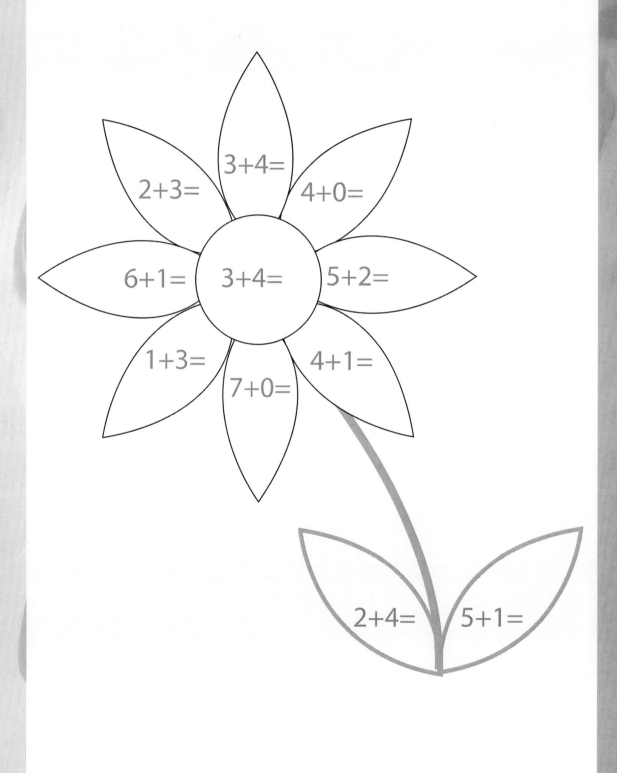

Boxes Game Square Grid

How Many Shapes?

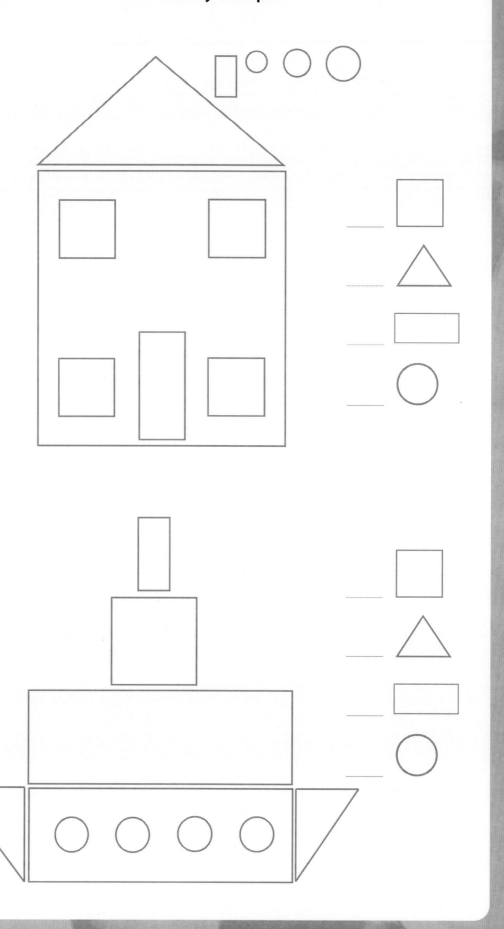

PAPER PLAY AND TECHNOLOGY CHALLENGES

Paper Play and Technology Challenges

Resource Box

A packet of A4 paper, sugar paper, tissue paper (white or coloured), gold foil, transparent paper.

Paper fasteners.

Activity cards.

Sellotape or masking tape.

Staplers.

Glue guns and ordinary glue.

Balsa wood.

Thick and thin card.

Scissors.

Crayons, pencils and pens.

Paint and brushes (optional).

String or wool.

Needle.

Compass.

Newspaper and old magazines.

Tape measure, metre stick or ruler.

When organising this wet play box, choose a selection of age appropriate activities for the children in your class to enjoy. There is a wide variety of things to do, most are simple to organise and all that is needed is a sheet of A4 paper. The only more complex activity is the Pom Pom, which is good for dexterity and fun to make. Children will find the activities entertaining and I'm sure you will hear lots of laughter.

Your activity box will need to be kept well stocked with the copiable pages.

Towers is easy to organise and will take up most of a lunchtime. Heads and Bodies and Consequences are fun, easy to make, with very little needed other than a pieces of A4 paper. The Positively You adaptation will bring a smile to most faces, help boost self-esteem and encourage children to value their strengths.

Do you remember making and playing Paper Fortune Tellers when you were a child? When children play with this game they fit their first two fingers into the pockets and then their partner takes turns picking from colours and numbers, eventually they get their fortune read, which can be amusing, inspiring or it could be a bit rude! The Paper Fortune Teller can be multi coloured, have pictures drawn on it or be decorated any way they want. One sheet of folded paper can keep kids busy for hours!

The paper snowflakes and table lantern provide hours of fun in the winter months and are particularly good to make at Christmas time.

The Origami elephant is easy to make and I have included a template at the back of this section to help. The word Origami comes from the Japanese word oru meaning 'folding', and kami meaning 'paper'. It is the traditional Japanese art of paper folding. The goal of this art is to create a representation of an object using geometric folds and crease patterns preferably without the use of gluing or cutting the paper, and using only one piece of paper.

Traditional Japanese origami is believed to have been practiced since the Edo era (1603–1867).

I have included a mask for making a Life Mask. This idea originated from death masks which were a wax or plaster cast of a mould taken from the face of a dead individual. Death masks were true portraits, although changes were occasionally made in the eyes of the mask to make it appear as though the subject were alive. They were used in days of old when relatives of people who had died had them made up as keepsakes of their loved ones.

To see some go to: http://www.liverpoolmuseums.org.uk/nof/top/deathmask.html

A life mask is different in that it is intended as something very positive and uplifting and as an opportunity to display a child's inner self, interests, hobbies, hopes and dreams.

The Rangoli, Islamic and Mehndi Patterns are beautiful patterns to colour in as you would like. Remember to keep these well stocked up in your wet play box.

Rangoli is a traditional form of folk art used for making colourful patterns on floors of houses and temples especially during important Hindu festivals like Divali and Holi. At Diwali, Hindus draw bright Rangoli patterns to encourage the goddess Lakshmi to enter their homes. The patterns are traditionally drawn with the fingers using flour, rice grains or coloured chalk.

Rangoli can be square, rectangular, circular or a mix of all three. They are often symmetrical. Rangoli motifs are usually taken from nature – peacocks, swans, mango, flowers and so on.

For more ideas go to: http://www.activityvillage.co.uk/rangoli.htm

Islamic design is based upon the repetition of symmetrical pattern. The basic unit can be repeated again and again to make a pattern which is both geometrical and rhythmical.

Mehndi is an art form which is widely practiced during festival times and to celebrate weddings. Complex or simple patterns are drawn on the hands and sometimes on the feet. These patterns are applied using henna paste (Mehndi) and usually last for a few days.

16. Towers

Age Range: 7-11
Ideal Number of Players: Teams of 3-6
Equipment Needed: Newspaper, sellotape or masking tape, scissors, tape measure or metre stick

What to Do

Students are divided into teams of 3-6. Each team has 20 minutes, which is usually most of the lunchtime, to build the highest tower possible using the resources provided.
The tower must stand long enough for it to be measured. An adult or rainbow play leader measures the towers and one team is declared the winner.
How did working in teams make this activity easier to accomplish than working alone?
How did working in a team make this activity harder to accomplish?
What is the advantage of working in a team?
What is the disadvantage of working in a team?

Rules

Players must only use the resources provided. The tower cannot be affixed to the ground, it needs to be free standing.
Make sure you allow enough time before play finishes to measure the tower and work out the winners.

Variations

Index cards can be used instead of newspaper.

17. Heads and Bodies

Age Range: 5-11
Ideal Number of Players: 4+
Equipment Needed: A piece of A4 paper for each player and pens or pencils

What to do

Each player draws a head on top of his piece of paper with a neck below and folds his paper over so that only a little of the neck is showing. At the command 'pass' he passes his paper to the player to his left, receiving in exchange one from the player on his right. Each player then draws a body onto the neck, finishing at the top of the legs. He then folds the paper again, leaving a little of the legs showing and exchanging papers as before.
Each payer adds legs and feet and folds the paper, leaving only a blank space showing and passes again.
Finally each player adds a name and folds the paper once more. The papers are then jumbled up. Each player chooses one and then unfolds it and they all look at the results together. It usually produces a lot of laughter!

Rules

Wait patiently until your players have finished drawing before you pass your papers on.

Variations

A variation of this game which I have always loved using in class is called 'Positively You'. Children write their name at the top of the paper, they then fold it over as above and pass the paper to the player on their left, receiving in exchange the folded paper from the player on their right. Players then write a positive statement about the person whose name is at the top. The player then folds the paper as in the game above and passes it on. The game continues until everyone in the group has written a positive statement about the person whose name is at the top of the paper. The game finishes when you receive your piece of paper back. All players then open out and read their own positive news statements. Lots of smiles and comments usually follow.

18. Consequences

Age Range: 5-11
Ideal Number Of Players: 4+
Equipment Needed: A piece of A4 paper for each player and pens or pencils

What to Do

This game is similar to heads and bodies, though involves drawing and writing.
Each player draws a picture at the top of his piece of paper and folds the paper over so that nobody can see the picture. At the command 'pass' he passes his paper to the player on his left, receiving in exchange one from the player on his right.
This player then peeks at the picture underneath and describes briefly in writing what he thinks that picture is of. He then folds the paper over and passes it to the person on his left. The next player then reads what the previous player had written and draws a picture of the item described.

The play continues with players often being uncertain what the picture is of and other players struggling to draw pictures to describe what is written.
Finally the papers are then jumbled up, each player chooses one and then unfolds it and they all look at the results together. It usually produces a lot of laughter!

Rules

Wait patiently until your players have finished drawing before you pass your papers on.

19. Paper Fortune Teller

Age Range: 7-11
Ideal Number of Players: 1+
Equipment Needed: Paper and pencils

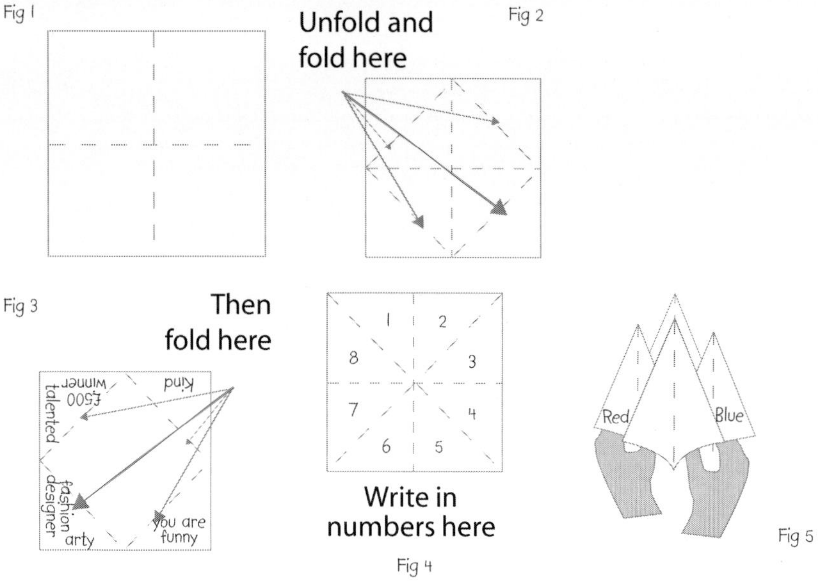

What to Do

Players take a squared piece of paper and fold it in half twice (Fig. 1). They then open it and crease the four corners into the centre (Fig.2). Next get them to turn it over and write fortunes round the corner of the edges (Fig. 3).

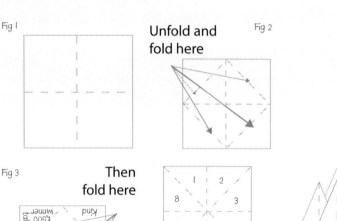

Fig 1
Fig 2 — Unfold and fold here
Fig 3 — Then fold here
Fig 4 — Write in numbers here
Fig 5

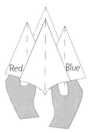

For example: You are funny, you are sporty, fashionable, kind, musical, funny, you just won a talent competition, you have been invited to appear on TV, you just won £500.00, you just won whatever job you want, you are a talented musician and so on. They then turn these new four corners into the centre and crease and mark numbers 1-8 on the flaps as in Fig. 4. Then get them to turn it over and write colours on the opposite side. Next get them to fold it in half, then open and fold in half the other way. Slip their two thumbs and two forefingers underneath the flaps facing them. (Fig. 5). They will find that by moving their fingers and thumbs they open the 'pyramids' in two directions, one showing numbers 1,2,6 and 7 and the other showing numbers 3,4,7 and 8.

Get them to ask a friend to choose a colour, after which they open and shut the pyramid according to the letters of that colour; for example, if Amber chose pink, the person with the fortune teller would open and close the pyramid 4 times, saying P-I-N-K, she then would ask her partner for a number between 1 and 4. If she chooses 3, she would open and shut the pyramid 3 times. She then would ask her to choose another number and again do the same thing. She would then ask her a third time to choose a number, turn back the corresponding flap and read her the 'fortune'.

Variations

There are lots of ways of adapting what is written on the fortune teller, many children colour the squares, draw pictures, or decorate them in any way they want.

20. Snowflakes and Stars

Age Range: 5-11
Ideal Number of Players: 1+
Equipment Needed: Scissors, compass or round plate, ordinary or transparent paper

What to Do

Draw a circle on a piece of paper using the compass or plate to draw around.
Cut the circle out, fold it in half and fold it in half again. Make sure that you smooth down the folds with your thumbnail.

Now cut small pieces out of the folded sides, for example, triangles, half circles and so on. Carefully unfold the paper to reveal the pattern you have created.

To make a star, cut a triangle into the round edge.

You can stick transparent paper behind the finished stars and snowflakes to make pretty window decorations. They can also be used as coasters for special occasions.

21. Table Lantern

Age Range: 6-11
Ideal Number Of Players: 1+
Equipment Needed: Paper or gold foil, glue, tape or a stapler, ruler, scissors

What to Do

Cut a strip of paper 20x12cm and fold it in half lengthwise, making a long rectangle or alternatively a piece of A4 paper will also work. Then, using a ruler, draw a horizontal line parallel to the edge of the long side, about 1cm below the (non-folded) edge.

To make this easier use the template on page 78.
Cut straight slits about 1cm apart into the paper from the folded edge to the drawn line.

- Unfold and glue, staple or sellotape the left and right edge strips together.

- Cut a strip of paper 15cm long and 2cm wide. Glue or staple this strip of paper across one end of the lantern. This will be the handle of the lantern.

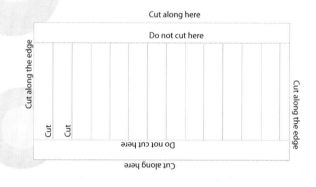
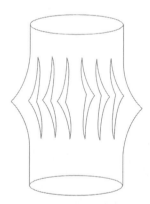

Variations

Make a lot of lanterns and string them along a length of yarn. Decorate your classroom! You can use A4 paper for a much bigger lantern.

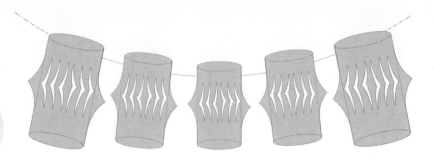

22. Origami – Make an Elephant

Age Range: 7-11
Ideal Number of Players: 1
Equipment Needed: A squared shape piece of paper or the template at the back of this section

What to Do

Figure 1

Using a squared piece of paper (20cm x 20cm – see page 79), create a kite shape by folding the square diagonally along line AC, then unfold and fold lines AB and AD over to line AC.

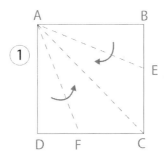

Figure 2

Fold line AE over to line AF.

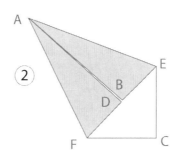

Figure 3.

Fold A over to the right, at new points N and O.

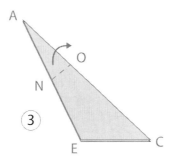

Figure 4 and Figure 5.

4. Place your fingers between opening MO and open out so that the elephant model at this stage appears as in figure 5.
5. Fold along the crease AO bringing both ends together.

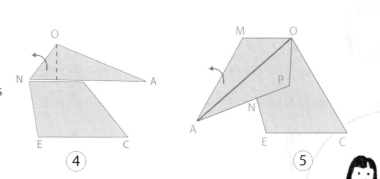

65

22. Origami – Make an Elephant (Continued)

Figure 6 and Figure 7.

Crease at points XX downwards, unfold (6) and then bring point A between the flaps (7).

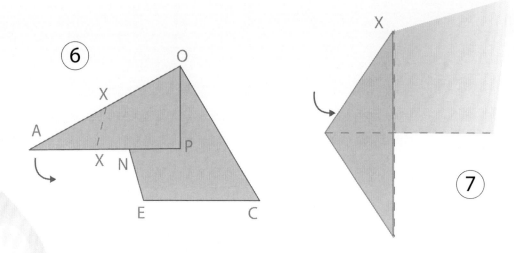

Figure 8 and figure 9

Cut away portions marked by the dotted lines and draw elephant features (8). Finished elephant (9).

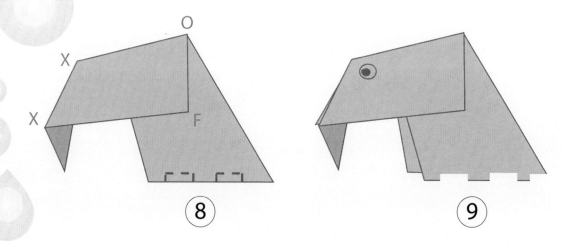

23. Make a Paper Bird

Age Range: 5-11
Ideal Number of Players: 1
Equipment Needed: Sugar paper – assorted colours, bird template (optional), scissors, drawing paper or tissue paper (white or coloured) crayons, string or wool

What to Do

Cut the sugar paper into bird shapes. Use the shapes on page 80 or invent your own.

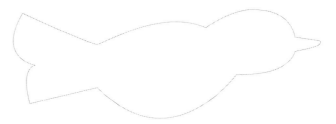

Cut a small slit in the body where the wings should be.

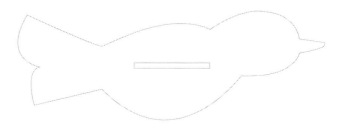

To make the wings, cut a small rectangle out of the drawing or tissue paper. If you are using tissue paper you can let the children colour the wings. Then fold the paper back and forwards, accordion style and slide this through the slit in the body. It should be a tight fit.
Spread the folded wings out. You can also glue or staple the top edges of the wings together so that they stay open. Attach a piece of string to the body at the top of the back.

Let the children 'fly' their birds by holding the string.

24. Pom Pom Balls

Age Range: 5-11
Ideal Number Of Players: 1 each
Equipment Needed: Thick wool, cardboard, large scissors, wool needle, compass

What to Do

Prepare the wool by cutting it into arm length strands. Keep these to the side or in a container.

Use the compass to draw onto the cardboard two doughnut-shaped rings for each pom pom. You can share the rings letting one child use them after another has finished. Cut a slit in each ring. This will allow you to slide the pom pom off when you are finished, so the ring can be re-used.

Give the children the two rings and an arm's length of wool. You may use a variety of colours to make a confetti coloured pom pom or just use one colour.

Demonstrate to the children how to wrap the wool around the ring, going through the centre hole and around the 'doughnut' part of the ring and continuing as so until there is little wool left. The last bit of wool can be tucked under the wrapped wool to keep it from unravelling.

Continue wrapping the strands of wool until the centre hole of the doughnut is completely filled up. You will know this when it is hard to push the wool through the centre hole. Tuck the last end under the other strands.

Using a large sharp pair of scissors, cut around the outside edge of the pom pom, keeping one blade between the two cardboard rings.

Using a heavy thread or doubled wool, tie the pom pom tightly through the middle of the two pieces of cardboard.

Slide the wool off the ring through the cut slits. Fluff up and trim the pom pom.

This activity will take up a whole playtime.

Variations

To add a bell, thread a wool needle with doubled wool, run it through the bells loop and then run the needle back through its own wool to anchor the bell to the wool. Then thread the needle up through the centre of the pom pom. Pull snugly, so the bell nestles in. Cut the thread and knot it so that a large loop is formed, you can then use this to hang the pom pom.

25. Make a Life Mask

Age Range: 5-11
Ideal Number of Players: 1 per person
Equipment Needed: Scissors, cardboard (approx 20.5x28cm), mask template (optional), old magazines, postcards, photographs, crayons and felt pens, paints (optional), paintbrush (optional) stapler, 26cm length of string

What to Do

Make a life mask that displays your inner self – your interests, talents, strengths, hobbies and dreams. Create your own shape or use one of the templates (page 81).

Cut holes in the card for the eyes, nose and mouth.

Then cut out a selection of pictures, words, phrases that represent the things that love from magazines, postcards and photographs. You may have poems or quotes that are special to you that you could add. You could use the computer to research and then print out your pictures, quotes or words that you find.

If you like sports you may like to cut out pictures of people playing netball, football, tennis and so on.

Do you have a pet?
Do you like to spend time in nature? If so go out and collect leaves and flowers to include on your mask. Also cut out words that describe you.

Once you have made a collection of words and pictures that describe you, create a collage with them on your mask, gluing them onto the card.

You can also use crayons, felt pens or paints to decorate the mask as well.

Some students like to cover every part of the mask, others like to have some spaces, it is up to you to make your mask as an expression of who you are.

Staple each end of the string to the back of the mask, making sure it fits your face, or you may want to hang it on a wall.

26. Make and Decorate a Cube

Age Range: 6-11
Ideal Number of Players: 1
Equipment Needed: Cube template, scissors, glue

What to Do

Cut out and decorate before glueing.

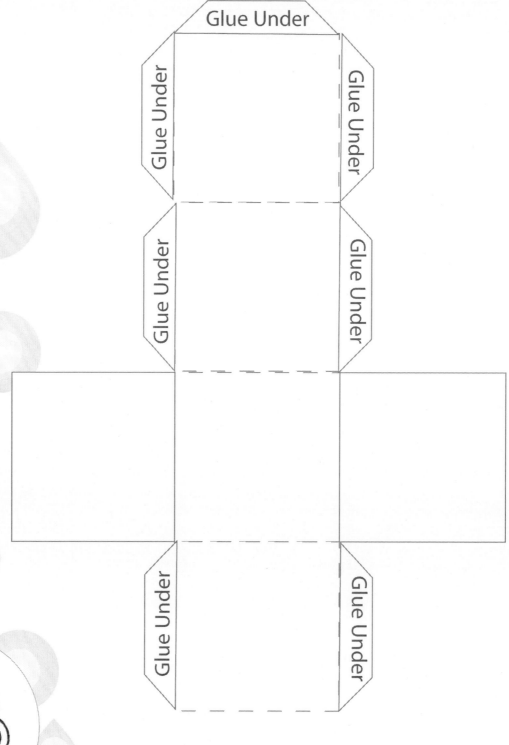

27. Elves Colouring In Sheet

28. Fishes Colouring In Sheet

29. Magical Colouring In Sheet

30. Isometric Dot Paper

Create your own unique patterns.

31. Rangoli Pattern 1

Rangoli is the traditional form of folk art used for making patterns on floors of houses and temples, especially during important Hindu festivals like Diwali and Holi. They welcome visitors and guests and bring happiness and tranquility around the household throughout the year. Colour Pattern 1 or complete Pattern 2 (page 82) or create your own pattern.

32. Islamic Pattern 1

Islamic design is based upon the repetition of symmetrical pattern. The basic unit can be repeated again and again to make a pattern which is both geometrical and rhymical. Either colour Pattern 1 or complete Pattern 2 (page 83) or create your own pattern.

TTI 101 Wet Playtime Games and Activities

33. Mehndi Patterns

Mehndi is an art form which is widely practiced during the festival times and to celebrate weddings. Complex or simple patterns are drawn on the hands and sometimes on feet. These patterns are applied using henna paste (mehndi) and usually last for a few days. Now trace around your own hand and make up a Mehndi pattern or complete page 84.

Table Lantern Template

Cut along the edge

Cut

Cut

Cut along here

Do not cut here

Do not cut here

Cut along here

Cut along the edge

Make an Elephant Template

Cut along the squares edge.

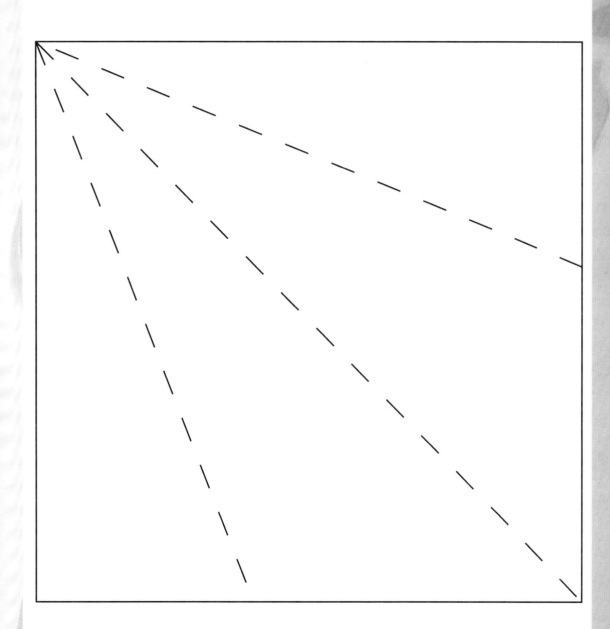

Paper Bird Template

Life Mask Template

Rangoli Pattern 2

Complete the Rangoli pattern.

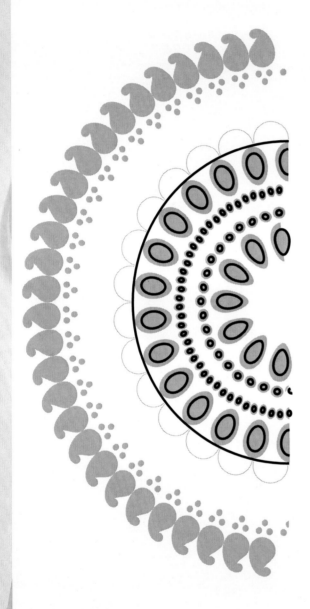

Islamic Pattern 2

Complete the Islamic pattern.

Mehndi Hand Template

Draw your own Mehndi pattern.

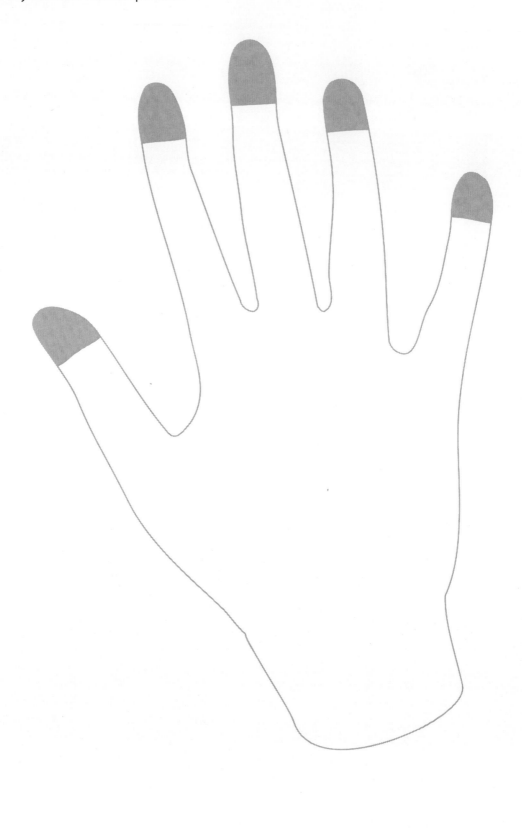

Paper Play and Technology Challenges

QUIZ AND PUZZLE ACTIVITIES

Quiz and Puzzle Activities

This section is filled with copiable resources that provide lots of entertainment for the lunch hour. Every classroom ideally should have a selection of these activities printed ready for a wet play day and stored in a wet play activity box.

However, many teachers tell me that they sometimes just aren't prepared for those rainy days and that's when they need a wet play activity book with a selection of activities and copiable resources that they can dip into at short notice or hand to an ever supportive lunchtime supervisor or classroom assistant to photocopy or print from the CD-ROM! So here you are, a resource to support you and make wet lunchtime organisation effortless.

There are some useful websites covering puzzles and quizzes in the Appendix.

Sudoku

Although Sudoku puzzles are made up of numbers, there is no maths involved. You must use logic to work out where the numbers go and that is what makes the puzzles fun. Every puzzle is different and once you get the hang of it, you may find yourself wanting to do more and more!

How to do Sudoku Puzzles

To do the age 5-7 Sudoku puzzle you must make every column, row and mini-grid contain the numbers 1, 2, 3 and 4 – one of each. With the 7-11 Sudoku every column, row and mini grid must contain the numbers 1, 2, 3, 4, 5 and 6. There is only one way to finish each puzzle and if you think carefully you will be able to work out the answer.

I have listed some useful sudoku websites in the Appendix.

34. General Trivia Quiz

Age Range: 7-11
Ideal Number of Players: 12
Equipment Needed: None

What to Do

Put the players into two teams.

Team A starts first and has to answer as many questions as possible. They score one point for every correct answer. Team B goes next. The winner is the team that scores the most points. Answer can be found on page 102. Ask the children to decide on bonus points if one team can't answer.

Ask two or three children to create some different quizzes for future wet playtimes.

Team A

1. Who wrote Harry Potter?
2. I have one dozen eggs. How many do I have?
3. What is the currency of Australia?
4. What is the capital of France?
5. What colour is a New York taxi?
6. Who wrote Matilda?
7. In Walt Disney's Jungle Book what type of animal was Bagheera?
8. What was the first strange animal that Alice saw in Wonderland?
9. Which children's novel begins with, 'All children except one grow up...'?
10. What colour were Dorothy's slippers in the Wizard of Oz?

Team B

11. Where did C. S. Lewis's wardrobe lead to?
12. In a leap year, how many days does February have?
13. How do you write the number nine in Roman numerals?
14. Which part of a plant makes most of the food it needs?
15. Water freezes at 0 degree Centigrade. True or false?
16. Rome is the capital of where?
17. Complete this TV programme saying. 'I'm a celebrity get me...'
18. In which city is the London Eye?
19. Where is Leeds Castle?
20. Who was the first man on the moon?

35. Colours Wordsearch

Age Range: 5-7
Ideal Number of Players: 1+
Equipment Needed: Pen or pencil

G	C	K	W	M	H	M	A	H	E	A	Z
Y	R	W	J	C	M	A	Y	E	H	C	T
D	Z	E	W	D	Q	N	Y	L	G	X	O
M	E	U	E	O	D	G	N	P	D	P	Y
N	B	R	E	N	L	I	E	R	F	S	B
E	G	N	A	R	O	L	T	U	J	M	R
I	N	D	I	G	O	E	E	P	L	B	O
E	T	I	H	W	L	Q	Y	Y	L	B	W
L	H	O	K	O	D	Z	M	A	K	A	N
S	I	M	I	I	G	P	C	W	N	L	E
H	U	V	E	Y	N	K	Y	G	I	B	F
Z	A	L	F	R	D	X	T	Q	P	S	V

Find the 12 colours listed below:

BLACK	GREEN
PINK	VIOLET
BLUE	INDIGO
PURPLE	WHITE
BROWN	ORANGE
RED	YELLOW

TTI 101 Wet Playtime Games and Activities

36. Months of the Year Worksearch

Age Range: 6-9
Ideal Number Of Players: 1+
Equipment Needed: Pen or pencil

```
O  L  J  Y  L  M  A  Y  B  X  W  R
C  A  J  R  B  I  I  G  K  J  E  O
T  E  T  A  X  H  R  L  A  B  E  S
O  R  T  U  K  K  W  P  M  U  C  I
B  P  E  R  N  L  T  E  A  E  Q  U
E  T  C  B  F  J  V  H  A  B  D  P
R  Z  N  E  M  O  A  U  E  K  W  G
B  D  X  F  N  E  G  N  N  L  O  I
H  C  R  A  M  U  T  L  U  W  Q  Y
W  S  A  X  S  I  P  P  J  A  L  L
M  L  G  T  U  Y  U  F  E  U  R  H
D  E  C  E  M  B  E  R  J  S  J  Y
```

Find the 12 months of the year listed below:

APRIL	AUGUST
DECEMBER	FEBRUARY
JANUARY	JULY
JUNE	MARCH
MAY	NOVEMBER
OCTOBER	SEPTEMBER

TTI 101 Wet Playtime Games and Activities

37. Friendship Wordsearch

Age Range: 7-11
Ideal Number of Players: 1+
Equipment Needed: Pen or pencil

F	I	H	G	A	E	N	C	O	U	R	A	G	E	F
F	N	E	K	C	W	O	W	T	E	Y	Y	D	W	A
R	S	L	J	K	K	X	P	G	N	N	D	B	F	I
I	I	P	V	N	B	N	N	N	L	O	Y	A	L	T
E	H	N	H	O	P	E	U	H	H	I	Z	W	R	H
N	R	Q	C	W	L	F	V	C	Y	T	A	E	Y	F
D	B	P	T	L	X	Z	T	Z	M	A	L	P	Z	U
S	O	O	A	E	U	F	O	R	G	I	V	E	M	L
L	H	H	H	G	W	S	C	K	A	C	R	M	E	U
U	C	A	S	E	L	P	I	B	Y	E	G	I	Q	F
F	S	P	R	M	R	N	L	V	R	R	U	Z	W	H
Y	B	R	G	E	D	E	N	A	E	P	L	N	I	T
A	E	T	A	N	O	I	S	S	A	P	M	O	C	U
L	R	E	H	T	E	G	O	T	F	A	K	C	K	R
P	A	E	L	U	F	P	L	E	H	O	Z	P	S	T

Find the 18 Friendship words listed below:

ACKNOWLEGEMENT	APPRECIATION	CHALLENGE
COMPASSIONATE	ENCOURAGE	FAITHFUL
FORGIVE	FRIENDS	FUNNY
HELPFUL	INCLUSIVE	KIND
LOYAL	PLAYFUL	RELIABLE
SHARE	TOGETHER	TRUTHFUL

38. Countries Wordsearch

Age Range: 7-11
Ideal Number of Players: 1+
Equipment Needed: Pen or pencil

```
S   V   E   W   M   N   A   D   K   X   O   A

Z   W   O   H   A   U   N   I   I   F   A   U

F   J   I   P   Q   A   I   E   D   U   F   S

A   R   A   T   L   G   N   G   S   N   U   T

F   J   A   L   Z   G   E   T   L   G   I   R

K   Y   O   N   L   E   R   R   N   E   Y   A

R   H   L   A   C   I   R   E   M   A   B   L

A   G   N   Z   A   E   S   L   L   A   B   I

M   D   N   A   L   O   P   Z   A   I   N   A

N   I   Y   T   U   R   K   E   Y   N   H   Y

E   Y   A   W   R   O   N   O   D   B   D   C

D   I   R   E   L   A   N   D   L   J   B   K
```

Find the 17 Countries listed below:

AMERICA	AUSTRALIA	AUSTRIA
BELGIUM	CHILE	DENMARK
ENGLAND	FRANCE	GERMANY
HOLLAND	INDIA	IRELAND
JAPAN	NORWAY	POLAND
SWITZERLAND	TURKEY	

39. World of Painting Wordsearch

Age Range: 7-11
Ideal Number of Players: 1+
Equipment Needed: Pen or pencil

```
M  Z  I  B  X  T  Y  L  F  V  A  L  P  A  W
V  O  A  H  L  E  A  S  E  L  P  A  J  B  G
N  O  I  T  I  B  I  H  X  E  I  O  R  N  G
W  O  Z  Q  O  A  C  D  X  Y  C  C  R  D  J
R  P  A  M  G  I  I  W  X  F  A  R  S  X  K
E  O  G  A  L  L  E  R  Y  Q  S  A  O  F  O
L  L  T  Y  N  R  E  D  O  M  O  H  B  W  E
E  I  R  C  S  T  I  F  N  I  S  C  O  E  Q
D  C  C  C  E  G  P  I  R  U  P  C  I  I  C
A  N  X  N  Z  L  M  A  R  A  A  P  L  H  E
Z  L  A  H  E  N  L  B  L  N  M  I  S  C  G
J  M  D  V  V  P  N  O  V  E  Y  E  B  T  J
U  U  L  M  S  P  X  A  C  X  T  D  J  E  U
X  K  W  K  W  K  S  I  R  G  X  T  K  K  F
R  Y  N  I  J  Z  H  R  U  T  J  U  E  S  M
```

Find the 15 world of painting words listed below:

ACRYLIC	BRUSH	CANVAS
CHARCOAL	COLLECTOR	EASEL
EXHIBITION	FRAME	GALLERY
MODERN	OILS	PALETTE
PENCIL	PICASO	SKETCH

40. Friendship Crossword

Age Range: 7-11
Ideal Number of Players: 1+
Equipment Needed: Pen or pencil

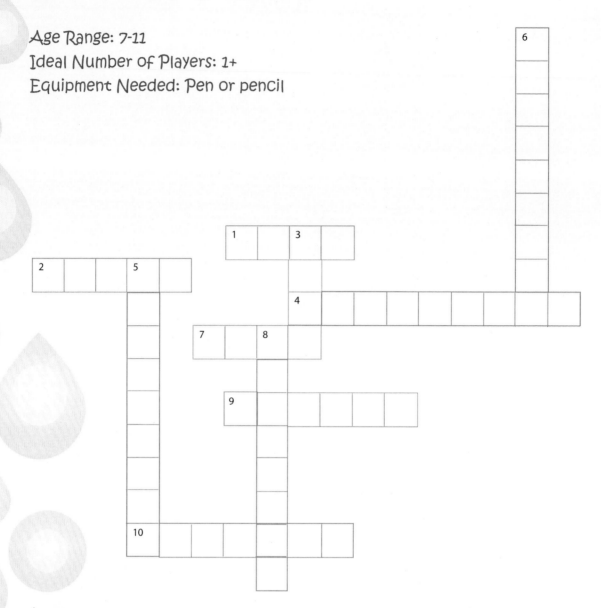

Across

1. When you are caring and helpful.
2. When you can rely on others.
4. When you work well together.
7. Monopoly is a .... that friends play.
9. Special and different.
10. Admiration for someone because of their qualities and achievements.

Down

3. Friendly and polite.
5. Staying at friends houses overnight.
6. Not the same.
8. You can say that people are polite and well ....

Answer can be found on page 103.

94

41. Mouse Maze

Age Range: 4-7
Ideal Number of Players: 1+
Equipment Needed: Pen or pencil

What to Do

Help the mouse get through the maze and find his piece of cheese.

42. Fishes Adding Up and Subtraction Colouring In

Age Range: 5-7
Ideal Number of Players: 1+
Equipment Needed: Pen or pencil, coloured pencils

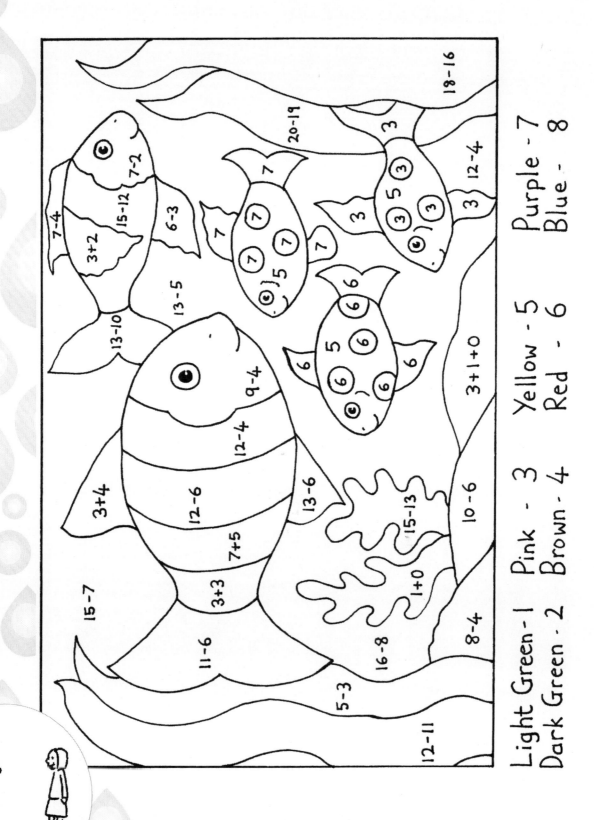

TTI 101 Wet Playtime Games and Activities

43. Magic Squares

Age Range: 7-11
Ideal Number of Players: 1+
Equipment Needed: Pen or pencil

What to Do

Can you make each line of the square add up to the number at the side of the square, whether you read it vertically, horizontally or diagonally?

	7	6
	5	

15

		6
	4	1

9

3		6
	5	

12

5		3
	2	

18

Can you find the magic number for this square and write it at the side?

2	9	4
	5	.

?

Answer can be found on page 104.

44. Sudoku

Age Range: 5-7
Ideal Number Of Players: 1+
Equipment Needed: Pen or pencil

What to Do

Every row, column and mini-grid must contain the numbers 1 through 4. Don't guess – use logic!

		3	
	4		
		1	
	2		

Answer can be found on page 105.

45. Sudoku

Every row, column and mini-grid must contain the numbers
1 through 6. Don't guess – use logic!

		2	4		
4					2
	2			3	
	4			6	
1					6
		3	5		

Answer can be found on page 106.

TTI 101 Wet Playtime Games and Activities

46. Squirrel Dot to Dot

Age Range: 5-7
Ideal Number of Players: 1
Equipment Needed: Pen or pencil

What to Do

Look at the numbers and join the dots to complete the picture.

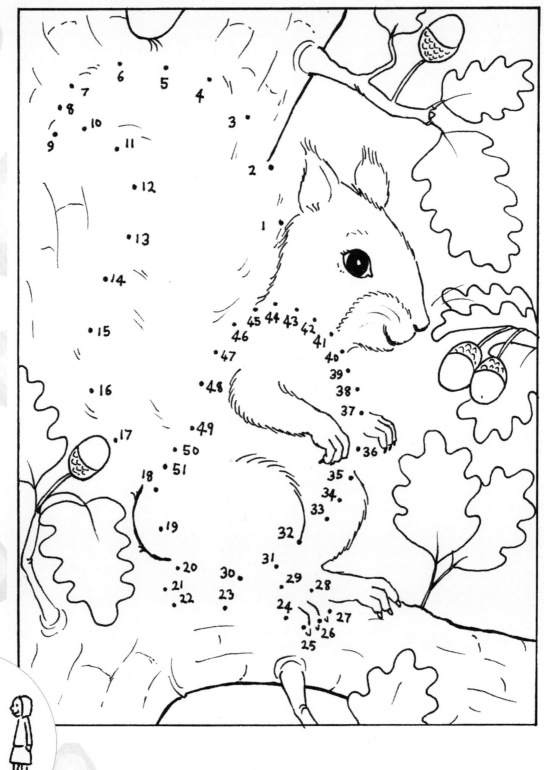

47. Frog Dot to Dot

Age Range: 5-7
Ideal Number of Players: 1
Equipment Needed: Pen or pencil

What to Do

Look at the numbers and join the dots to complete the picture.

Quiz Answers

1. Who wrote Harry Potter? J. K. Rowling

2. I have one dozen eggs how many do I have? 12

3. What is the currency of Australia? Australian dollars

4. What is the capital of France? Paris

5. What colour is a New York taxi? Yellow

6. Who wrote Matilda? Ronald Dahl

7. In Walt Disney's Jungle Book what type of animal was Bagheera? Panther

8. What was the first strange animal that Alice saw in Wonderland? White Rabbit

9. Which children's novel begins with, 'All children except one grow up...'? Peter Pan

10. What colour were Dorothy's slippers in the Wizard of Oz? Ruby red

11. Where did C. S. Lewis's wardrobe lead to? Narnia

12. In a leap year, how many days does February have? 29

13. How do you write the number nine in Roman numerals? IX

14. Which part of a plant makes most of the food it needs? Leaves

15. Water freezes at 0 degree Centigrade. True or False? True

16. Rome is the capital of where? Italy

17. Complete this TV programme saying, 'I'm a celebrity get me...' Out of here

18. In which city is the London Eye? London

19. Where is Leeds Castle? Maidstone, Kent.

20. Who was the first man on the moon? Neil Armstrong

Quiz and Puzzle Activities

Friendship Crossword Answers

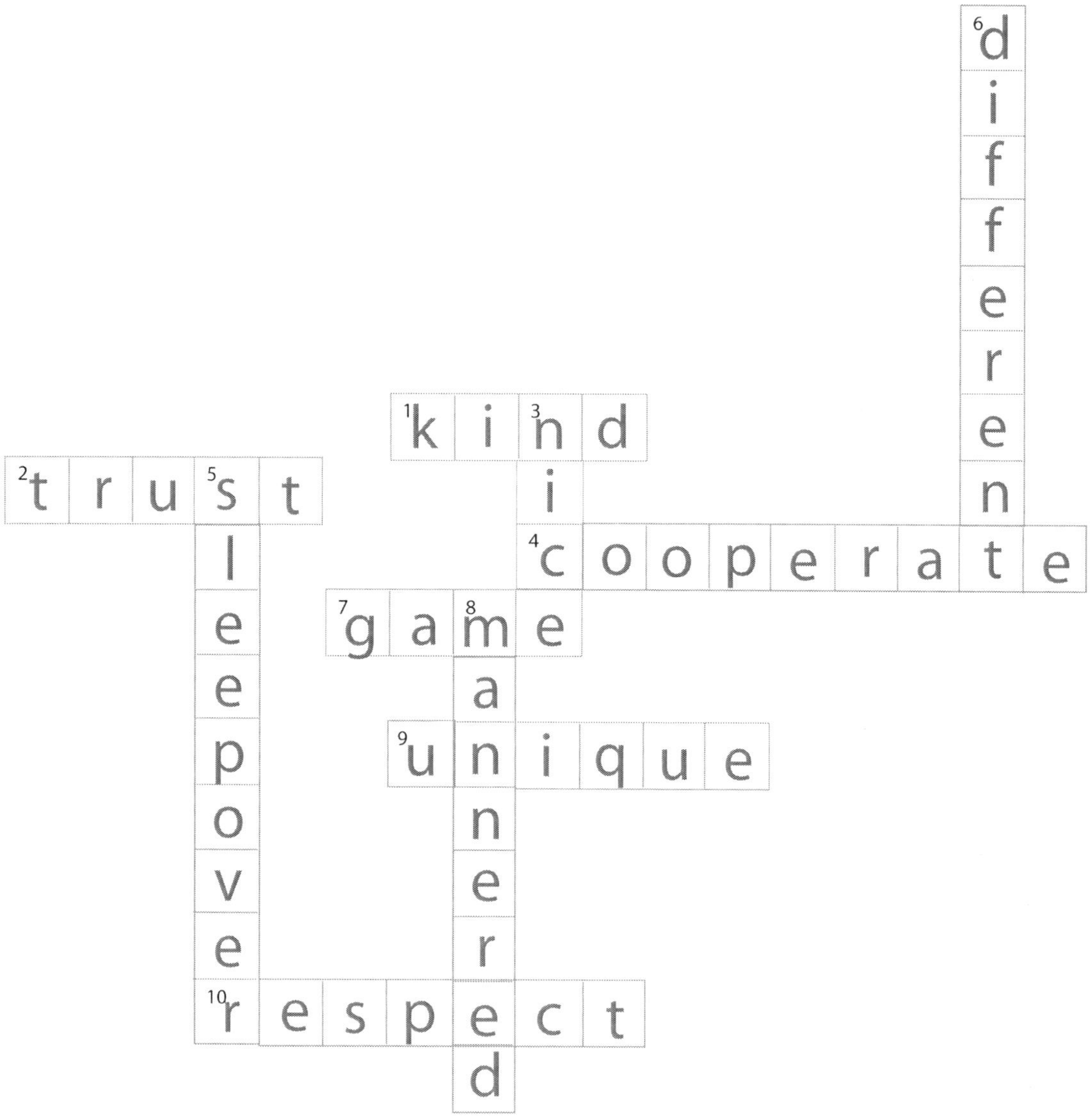

1 kind
2 trust
3 nice
4 cooperate
5 sleepover
6 different
7 game
8 mannered
9 unique
10 respect

Magic Square Answers

Can you make each line of the square add up to the number at the side of the square, whether you read it vertically, horizontally or diagonally?

2	7	6
9	5	1
4	3	8

15

5	2	2
0	3	6
4	4	1

9

3	3	6
7	4	1
2	5	5

12

5	10	3
4	6	8
9	2	7

18

Can you find the magic number for this square and write it at the side?

2	9	4
7	5	3
6	1	8

15

Quiz and Puzzle Activities

Sudoku 4-7 Answers

2	1	3	4
3	4	2	1
4	3	1	2
1	2	4	3

Sudoku 7-11 Answers

6	1	2	4	5	3
4	3	5	6	1	2
5	2	6	1	3	4
3	4	1	2	6	5
1	5	4	3	2	6
2	6	3	5	4	1

Quiz and Puzzle Activities

ACTIVE GAMES

Circle Games
Parachute Games
Active Games for Letting Off Steam
Singing, Rhyming and Dancing Games

CIRCLE GAMES

Circle Games

'The most exciting breakthrough of the 21st century will not occur because of technology but because of an expanded concept of what it means to be human.'

John Naisbitt, Futurist and author of Megatrends (1984)

Groups of people and children have been meeting in circles for thousands of years from the Native American Indians who passed around the peace pipe, to the Aboriginal and Maori tribes who have told stories with wise and meaningful metaphors. The circle is symbolic of unity, democracy, cooperation and deep respect. As one child on one of my Circle Time courses recently commented, 'There is no head of a circle. So collectively we work together, as a team.'

Thus when children sit in circles and play games they are building a whole host of personal and social competencies, for example, taking turns, listening to one another, self-control, sharing, thinking, cooperation, the ability to work as a team and so on.

Many of the games in this section meet the goals of the SEAL primary national strategy and support children in building social skills, greater self-awareness, empathy, and the skills to help them to manage their feelings. When playing games like the Compliments Game, children become aware of how their words affect others and in this way they also develop empathy and self-awareness.

This section includes fifteen circle games, which are also often referred to as ring games and are great whole-class or small group wet lunchtime activities.

All the games build social, emotional and behavioural skills.

Buzz is a great mental maths game and requires concentration and quick thinking. The Hat Game is ideal for foundation stage children. It requires cooperation, turn taking and team work. The Spider's Web is a team game that is creative, builds imagination, cooperation and memory. Conductor of the Orchestra is a game I have been playing for years in my Circle Times and one that children always love. Swap Places If… involves lots of movement. Human Knot is an active game which requires smart thinking and getting oneself in and out of knots. Big Fish Small Fish is fun, energising and can be very confusing, so make sure you are concentrating. The Compliments Game is a feel good game which builds friendship, self-esteem, empathy and self-awareness. The Story Chain is a creative group game that fosters imagination and builds cooperation and team skills. Heads Down Thumbs Up is a good calming down game at the end of a busy lunchtime. Mousetrap is the most lively and active out of all the games in this section. Who's Under the Blanket is a great favourite with foundation stage children as is When the North Wind Blows which can be played as a non-competitive or competitive game and is good for all ages. Sausages is one of the funniest games I know and will fill your classroom with lots of laughter. The Feelings Game helps children become more self-aware, relate to others and build empathy. It also supports them in developing a vocabulary of emotion.

Enjoy these circle games in your wet breaks.

48. Buzz

Age Range: 8-12
Ideal Number of Players: 6+
Equipment Needed: Pencil and paper for scoring

What to Do

This is a great children's mental maths game. It helps if children already know their times tables, although it is great practice for those wanting to boost their times tables knowledge.
Players should stand or sit in a circle. One person is chosen to start the game and players take turns around the circle counting in sequence from one. Play goes clockwise but this is where the game gets interesting.

If the number is divisible by seven or the number has the digit seven in it, the number is replaced by the word 'buzz!'. Play sounds like this: 'one, two, three, four, five, six, buzz! eight, nine' and so on. The numbers 14, 17, 21, 27, 28 would be the next ones to be buzzed.

When they reach the 70's all numbers are buzzed. For example, instead of saying 71, a player would say buzz,

Any number that is a multiple of seven and has a seven in it, for example, 70 and 77, gets a double buzz. So 70 and 77, would instead be buzz, buzz.

Play continues at as fast a pace as possible. If a player hesitates for too long or makes a mistake, such as missing their 'buzz' turn or saying 'buzz' when it isn't their turn then they get a penalty point and the game restarts from one again.

The game continues until they reach 100. The player with the fewest penalty points is the winner.

Variations

Instead of multiples of seven you can do multiples of five.

You can add multiples of five to the game and when you land on a multiple of five or a digit with five in it, you say 'fizz'. This game is then called 'fizz-buzz'.

112

49. The Hat Game

Age Range: 4-7
Ideal Number of Players: 10+
Equipment Needed: Two hats, for example, policeman's, fireman's, and music

What to Do

Take two hats into the circle with a CD or MP3 player and music. The game is played as musical hats.

Start with one of the hats and introduce the hat. Have a discussion about who wears a hat like this, what they do in their job and so on. The players in the circle then agree on an action that depicts the job that the 'hat wearer' does. For example, the fireman might have a hose and make whooshing noises to put out the fire. The policeman might lift his hat and say, 'Can I help you?' Try to avoid negative connotations of policemen rounding up robbers and jailing them!

The music starts and the first hat is passed from child to child round the circle. When the music stops, the child who has the hat puts it on and starts the action. All the rest of the group join her in the action. Then the music starts again. After a while introduce the second hat and then have two hats going round the circle and both the actions are done one after the other when the music stops.

Rules

Listen to one another and the music. Concentrate. Everyone can have a turn.

50. The Spiders Web Game

Age Range: 5-11
Ideal Number Of Players: 10+
Equipment Needed: Objects – shell, teddy, tiny toy and so on, ball of string or wool.

What to Do

Use the idea of having an imaginary treasure chest to introduce a theme, for example, a shell from the seaside, a tiny toy, a piece of tinsel, a pirates eye patch or treasure map. Have a discussion about the object and its significance.

The aim of the game is for the children to throw the ball of string from one to another calling out something to do with the theme when the string is caught. Over time each child is linked via the spiders web.

For example, the theme might be the seaside. The first child might begin with something that they think of when they think of the seaside, such as 'sand'. They hold the end of the string, then it is passed to another child who might say 'donkeys' and then to another 'water' and so on. As you continue, the ball of string unwinds and each child holds a bit until you have a made a web of ideas that link the group together.

The leader then rolls up the ball of string by recalling each child's contribution in reverse order. Players help the leader to remember what they said and they all help one another.

Variations

The above game can be played using names so that you end up with a web of friendships.

51. Conductor of the Orchestra

Age Range: 5-11
Ideal Number of Players: 10+
Equipment Needed: None

What to Do

Players sit in a circle and one person is chosen to be the detective. This person then leaves the room

A conductor is then chosen. This person decides on an action and beat. For example, clapping hands, clicking fingers, tapping head and everyone copies them.

The detective is then brought in and stands in the centre of the circle and moves around from that centre. He tries to guess who the conductor is. He has three guesses.

If he guesses correctly he can stay in again, otherwise a new conductor and detective are chosen.

Rules

The conductor must change the beat regularly. Players are not to look in the conductors direction. Players must copy the conductor, not make up any of their own actions to trick the detective.

Variations

Encourage the conductor to be creative with his actions. Sound and voices can also be used.

52. Swap Places If...

Age Range: 5-11
Ideal Number Of Players: 10+
Equipment Needed: Coloured labels

What to Do

Ask the children to sit in a circle.

With young children give them a coloured label with their name on. This means that when you play swap places, you can use the colours as well as the children's names.

You can also put number symbols up to five on the label so that they can use the numbers too.

Then you can have instructions such as:
'All reds hop across the circle and change places.'
'All greens walk across the circle, shake someone's hand and change places.'
'All two's stand on one leg and then change places.'

All variations on the above games develop listening, concentration and following instructions while giving the child a moment of focused attention.

Rules

Encourage children to cross the circle and change places

116

53. Human Knot

Age Range: 5-11
Ideal Number of Players: 5-15. For groups 'developing' cooperation skills, smaller groups of 6-8 work well.
Equipment Needed: None

What to Do

Players start by making a standing circle.

All players put their hands in the middle and with one hand they grab the hand of someone opposite and with the other they grab the hand of a different player. In this way they make a human knot.

The aim of the game is for the group to untangle themselves without unlinking hands. This can take up to 5-10 minutes.

Rules

Make sure they don't grab the hand of someone standing either side of them.

Variations

This version involves the holding of quoit instead of hands! All players are given a quoit and instead of holding their partners hand they hold their quoit. This is particularly good with Year 5's and 6's.

The game can be played verbally or silently.

Set a time limit.

54. Big Fish Small Fish

Age Range: 5-11
Ideal Number Of Players: 10+
Equipment Needed: None

What to Do

This is a fun energising game. Everyone sits in a circle. The leader tells the players that they are going to pass a pattern along the circle. The person who starts says, 'Big Fish,' and holds both their hands in front of them about three inches or ten centimeters apart. The next player can chose to pass the 'big fish' hand movement to the next person in the circle or they can choose to change the action to small fish.

If you say, 'Small Fish,' the player holds both hands in front of them, about 15 inches or 50 centimeters apart. When this is done, the direction changes.

Players that miss, for example, say 'Small Fish' and keep their hands too close together or say 'Big Fish' and move hands wide, do a forfeit or die with a loud noise.

Rules

Remember that this is a trick game and that small fish hand movements are with wide hands apart and big fish is small hands apart.

55. The Compliments Game

Age Range: 5-11
Ideal Number Of Players: 10+
Equipment Needed: None

What to Do

The children sit in a circle and the leader asks the class the question, 'Who wants to be complimented today?'

The children can show by raising their hands. This will make it a bit more interactive. The leader must ensure that each child has a turn.

The leader will select one child and ask her to leave the classroom. The leader then asks the rest of the class to say something good about the child who has left.

For example, 'Esther is very kind, has lovely eyes and is a good athlete.'

The leader makes a list of all the compliments and the names of the students who said them.

The child is then called back to the classroom. The leader reads all the compliments to the child with the names of the authors.

The leader should ask the class to give the child a round of applause.

This game creates a friendly atmosphere in the classroom.

Rules

Do this over various sessions if the group is very large. Keep a record of who has had a compliment paid to them to ensure that all children are selected.

56. The Story Chain

Age Range: 5-11
Ideal Number of Players: 5+
Equipment Needed: None

What to Do

This is a story telling game that can be played with all children sitting in a circle.

One person starts by telling a story, as exciting as possible, and breaks off in the middle of a sentence. Either the next person in a clockwise direction must go on with the story, or someone the first story teller chooses.

When the second story teller has had a turn, he stops suddenly to let someone else continue.

The story chain continues with everyone having a go and the final player creating an exciting end to the story.

120

57. Heads Down, Thumbs Up

Age Range: 5-11
Ideal Number of Players: 10+
Equipment Needed: None

What to Do

In this game the class or group of children can sit at their desks or tables with their eyes closed.

Two children are chosen to stand up and all the others put their heads down with their eyes closed and thumbs sticking up.

The two left standing must then creep around the desks and gently touch one person each on the thumb.

Everyone is then told to open their eyes and the children who were touched stand up and try to guess which child touched them.

If they get it right the children swap places, if not the children have another go.

58. Mousetrap

Age Range: 6-11
Ideal Number of Players: 15+
Equipment Needed: None

What to Do

10 or more players form a 'trap' by joining their hands in a circle with their arms up. The other remaining players are mice.

One player is chosen to be the cat and stands in the middle covering her eyes.

The mice run in and out of the mousetrap as the players forming the 'trap' randomly raise and lower their arms.

In the meantime, the cat counts silently to 20. On the count of 20 the cat yells, 'Snap!' and opens her eyes. The mousetrap players quickly lower their arms trapping some of the mice. These mice then join the circle of mousetrap players.

The goal is to be the last uncaught mouse who then becomes the cat.

59. Who's Under the Blanket

Age Range: 4-5
Ideal Number of Players: 6+
Equipment Needed: A large size blanket

What to Do

This game is always a favourite with early years children.

It is great for learning to take turns, learning each other's name, for the child to learn his whole name and to not be afraid when hiding alone. However, if the child is too afraid to hide underneath the blanket, you can change it to, 'Who's that hiding behind the blanket?'

The children sit around in a circle with their eyes closed whilst the play leader selects a child to sit in the middle of the circle. The play leader covers him over with the blanket. This player doesn't need to close their eyes.

Everyone sings (to the tune of One little, Two little, Three little Indians):

Who's that hiding underneath the blanket?

Who's that hiding underneath the blanket?

Who's that hiding underneath the blanket?

Let us guess your name!

Players then take it in turns guessing who is under the blanket and the person under the blanket replies in a disguised voice with either yes or no. The player who guesses correctly replaces the person under the blanket and the game starts again.

60. When the North Wind Blows

Age Range: 5-11
Ideal Number Of Players: 10+
Equipment Needed: None

What to Do

The children sit in a circle. One person is nominated to be the leader and stands in the middle of the circle.

The leader then calls out, 'When the north wind blows...' and then gives directions as to what she would like the players to do and they move to her instructions, usually changing places and moving to a different part of the circle. For example, 'When the north wind blows everyone must skip to another seat,', 'When the north wind blows you all become tiny mice and move to a different seat.'

This game can continue in a non-competitive way.

Variations

You can remove a seat and when the leader calls, 'When the north wind blows...' players move in the assigned way and find a seat as quickly as possible.

Players cannot sit in the seat next to them or in the same seat. The leader also has to find a seat. Whoever is left without a seat becomes the new leader and the game starts again.

Alternatively, if you are in the middle more than three times then you are out of the game.

124

61. Sausages

Age Range: 5-11
Ideal Number of Players: 12+
Equipment Needed: None

What to Do

This is a fun game to play and creates lots of merriment and laughter.

Someone is chosen to be 'on' from among the players and the aim of the game is for the other players to fire questions at him. These should be personal questions about school, holidays, favourite activities, names of teachers, anything to do with himself in fact. To every question the chosen person has to answer; 'sausages'.

So the game goes something like this:

Question: 'What's your favourite colour?'
Answer: 'Sausages'

Question: 'What do you call your bike?'
Answer: 'Sausages'

Questions: 'What's your brother's name?'
Answer: 'Sausages'

The chosen person has to keep a perfectly straight face throughout the game however ridiculous the answer sounds. Any giggle, any smile, any rolling on the floor in fits of laughter, the person is out and a new person is chosen.

Of course there is nothing to prevent all the others players from laughing and giggling as much as they like – it just makes the game so much more difficult for the person who can only say sausages.

Rules

Players are not to interrupt or help the player who is 'on'.

Variations

In another version of this game, players say, 'grannies green undies' instead of sausages.

62. The Feelings Game

Age Range: 5-11
Ideal Number of Players: 12+
Equipment Needed: Beanbag

What to Do

Players stand in a circle.

One person holds the beanbag. They throw the beanbag to someone across the circle who catches it and at the same time the thrower says a feeling which may, for instance, be happy. Everyone then mimes a happy feeling whilst staying in their place within the circle. The person who has caught the beanbag then throws the beanbag to another person within the circle and this time chooses a different feeling which may be sad. The game continues with different feelings being expressed by the group throughout the game. Remember to finish with a positive feeling.

Possible feelings:

- Scared.
- Angry.
- Excited.
- Bored.
- Jealous.
- Frightened.
- Confused.
- Awe and wonder.

Debrief of the game may include questions which ask:

- What did you notice about yourself when you played this game?
- Did your inner feelings change when you adopted the different feelings states?

Rules

Players are to be respectful of each others different feelings states and how feelings can effect us differently.

Variations

Instead of the group miming the feeling, the only person who mimes is the person who receives the beanbag. An extra beanbag can be added for fun and then two players have to mime.

PARACHUTE GAMES

Parachute Games

Parachute games are ideal for letting off steam and having fun on rainy days. Ideally they can be played in a hall with a large parachute or in a classroom with a smaller one.

The parachute was originally used in the late 18th Century to support people in falling safely from the sky. During wartime it was a particularly useful aid. Polish aviator Jodaki Kuparaento was the first to use a parachute as an emergency lifesaving device on July 24th 1808, when he jumped from a balloon that was on fire. Since his first jump to safety, parachutes have saved thousands of lives. In the 1960's many parachutes could be found in army and navy surplus stores and it was during this time that, '…many playful pioneers' found the opportunity and inspiration to create new recreational and physical education activities,' Le Fevre D (2006).

I was lucky enough in the 1990's to be given an ex air force wartime parachute by Mildred Masheder, wellknown for her work on cooperative group games. It was my first parachute and is made of a strong silk. The children and adults I have worked with over the years have had great fun playing with it.

Today there are many parachute makers who make parachutes specifically to play games with on the ground. I have included details in the Appendix of some companies.

The first few games in this section are intended to warm the children up and get them used to using a parachute. These games also help you to reinforce some of the basic skills and ground rules. The next games are very physically active and towards the end of the section the final games are intended to help children calm down at the end of wet playtime or when things get a little fraught!

All games are great fun, encourage light physical fitness, cooperative, non-competitive play and reinforce turn-taking, sharing and teamwork.

Terms

The parachute is sometimes referred to as the chute or canopy.

Rules

When starting the games care and consideration needs to be taken in explaining some basic rules to the children in order that you and they get the maximum fun out of the activities. We also need to make sure that children are safe and don't get hurt.

If you begin each session explaining some basic rules for the parachute games then the risk of injury will be reduced.

- Ask the children to remove their shoes before playing with the parachute.
- Encourage the children to space themselves around the parachute evenly so that there are no large gaps.
- Ensure the children hold the parachute with both hands with the thumb and fingers on top.
- The children should take care of those on either side as elbows can cause injury.
- Children are to be respectful of the parachute and not pull too hard or kick it.

- Inform the children that you will only select them as the game leader if they are sitting down quietly and not shouting out.

- If the parachute has a hole in the middle then please ensure that the children know it is dangerous to place their head through the centre.

Ages

Parachute games are for all age children and even adults. However you will need to evaluate each game against the age of the children, taking into consideration the level of risk and the complexity of instructions needed for some games.

Numbers

Obviously the larger the parachute the more children can participate. For example, a five meter parachute will be large enough for about 20 children. A seven meter parachute is ideal for the average class. For a small number of children a three meter parachute is ideal.

63. Mushroom

Age Range: 5-11
Ideal Number of Players: 10+
Equipment Needed: Parachute

What to Do

When someone shouts, 'One, two, three mushroom,' the children all rise up to full height with arms above their head to inflate the parachute. A giant mushroom is formed.

Have the players stand still and watch as the parachute settles slowly to the ground.

The children squat down and hold the parachute taut on the ground.
Players take it in turn to call out, 'One, two, three mushroom.'

Rules

Encourage the children to listen carefully to instructions.

Variations

Instead of 'One, two, three mushroom' the player may call out the name of any fruit or vegetable, for example, carrots, potatoes, broccoli and then 'mushroom'.

Floating Mushroom – the same as mushroom except on mushroom, everyone releases the parachute at the same time (ideally!) and the parachute floats up to the sky!

64. Mongolian Tent

Age Range: 5-11
Ideal Number of Players: 12+
Equipment Needed: Parachute

What to Do

The children squat down and hold the parachute taut on the ground.

When someone shouts, 'One, two, three mushroom,' the children all rise up to full height with their arms above their head to inflate the parachute over their heads.

As the parachute starts to make a giant, billowing mushroom effect, all the players pull the parachute behind their heads, backs and bottom and sit inside the parachute.

They keep in position by sitting on the edge of the parachute and leaning against the 'walls'.

Variations

Chinese Whispers can be played whilst the children are under the mushroom. To play this the children remain under the mushroom while one person is named the leader. This person secretly whispers a sentence such as, 'My cats name is Fluffy,' to the person next to her and this sentence continues around the circle until it reaches the last person who then recites out the sentence she has heard.

The leader verifies if the sentence is accurate or not – generally there are inaccuracies and sometimes players purposefully change the sentence along the way!

The game continues with a new leader.

65. Faces

Age Range: 5-11
Ideal Number of Players: 10+
Equipment Needed: Parachute

What to Do

The aim of this game is to develop confidence, good behaviour, listening to instructions and having fun.

Children gather around the parachute. The leader introduces facial expressions.

Children 'Mushroom' the parachute (see previous game). As it goes up they smile at one another underneath it. As it comes down, they have to be serious over the top. The children are changing their emotional expression.

Encourage them to notice how it looks and feels to express sadness, anger, laughter and fun and so on.

Then get them to wave with their left hands and right hands under the parachute as it goes up.

Later you can get them to swap places underneath the parachute by calling two names.

66. Fruit Salad

Age Range: 5-11
Ideal Number of Players: 10+
Equipment Needed: Parachute, optional Fruit Salad Cards.

What to Do

Children sit in a circle around the parachute. One person is nominated to be the leader.

The leader then gives the first three children the name of a fruit, for example, apple, orange, banana, then continues giving the same fruit names to the rest of the children around the circle.

The leader then calls out, 'One two three,' and the players mushroom the parachute. She then calls out the name of a fruit, for example, 'apple' and all the apples then quickly move places across the circle.

Another option is to call 'fruit salad' which means everyone must move. This can prove interesting and chaotic when using a parachute, though is great fun!

The game continues with a new leader eventually being chosen.

Rules

Children cannot move to the place next to them or go back to the same place.

Variations

Very young children may initially find it easier to use the fruit salad pictures on page 144. Each child is given a picture of a fruit as opposed to having to remember the fruit name. Ideally play leaders will have prepared these in advance. They can copy the pictures onto card and then laminate them. These can then be kept in the wet play box.

Instead of fruits the leader may want to call, 'Anyone who likes...' Then different categories can be selected such as colours, food, clothes, pets and so on.

134

67. Wink Murder

Age Range: 5-11
Ideal Number of Players: 12+
Equipment Needed: Parachute

What to Do

All the children sit in a circle around the parachute with their feet tucked under it. One person is chosen to be a detective.

If this game is being played in a classroom or hall the detective is normally asked to leave the room. Alternatively they can be asked to wear a blindfold.

While the detective is away or blindfolded, a person is secretly chosen to be the murderer.

Once this is done the detective is then called back or their blindfold is taken off and they are asked to stand in the centre of the parachute.

The murderer then proceeds to try and put the players to sleep by winking at them without the detective seeing.

Any players winked at must pretend that they are dying and slide under the parachute. Players tend to be very dramatic and make lots of noise, writhe on the floor, make their last requests and so on.

The detectives job is to guess who the murderer is before all the players are killed! The detective has three guesses.

Rules

Players are encouraged not to look at the murderer, which would let the detective know who it is.

68. Washing Machine

Age Range: 7-11
Ideal Number Of Players: 8+
Equipment Needed: Parachute

What to Do

On the count of three children raise their arms, lifting the parachute over their heads, pulling the parachute behind them.

They then sit down with their bottoms on the edge of the chute. The children should now be inside the chute.

Ask them then to start rocking from left – forward – right.

136

69. Cat and Mouse

Age Range: 7-11
Ideal Number of Players: 8+
Equipment Needed: Parachute

What to Do

A cat and mouse are chosen.

All players hold the chute stretched out quite close to the ground. The mouse goes underneath and the cat crawls on top and tries to hunt and tag the mouse.

The rest of the group try to hide the mouse by moving the chute up and down.

Rules

To avoid children getting hurt, make sure that the cat is crawling on all fours and not running upright. Make sure their shoes are off.

Variations

You may want to call them different animal names.

70. Popcorn

Age Range: 5-11
Ideal Number Of Players: 8+
Equipment Needed: Parachute

What to Do

Place a number of beanbags (or other objects) on the parachute. Everyone shakes the parachute to make them rise like popcorn.

71. Sharks

Age Range: 5-11
Ideal Number of Players: 12+
Equipment Needed: Parachute

What to Do

Everyone sits on the ground with their legs stretched out under the parachute and the parachute held at chest height. One or two children crawl around underneath and are 'sharks'. They quietly grab the legs of anyone around the perimeter, with many blood-curdling screams, and pull them under the canopy.

The shark now swaps places with their victim.

72. Eye Contact

Age Range: 6-11
Ideal Number of Players: 12+
Equipment Needed: Parachute

What to Do

Ask the children to play mushroom.

The children squat down and hold the parachute taut on the ground.

When someone shouts, 'One, two, three mushroom' the children all rise up to full height with arms above their head to inflate the parachute over their heads. A giant mushroom is formed.

On the next occasions when the player calls out 'One, two, three mushroom' players make eye contact with someone across the room and then swap places.

Rules

This game involves team work and players cooperating and working together.

140

73. Sleeping Lions

Age Range: 4-11
Ideal Number of Players: 10+
Equipment Needed: Parachute

What to Do

This game is to be played at the end of more active parachute games, for example, after playing Mushroom and Fruit Salad.

Ask the children to lie on the floor with their eyes closed and the parachute covering their body, but not their head and face.

Tell them that they are going to be sleeping lions and have to stay very still.

Choose a child to be the hunter or an adult can assume this role.

The hunters walk around the room and attempt to try and get the lions to move by talking to them or making faces at them or just standing above them.

Rules

The hunter is not allowed to touch the lions.

Any lion who moves is out of the game and has to go and sit at the side of the room. The last sleeping lion left in the game is the winner.

141

74. Row, Row, Row Your Boat

Age Range: 5-11
Ideal Number of Players: 8+
Equipment Needed: Parachute

What to Do

Players sit on the floor around the parachute with their feet and legs under the parachute.

They take hold of the parachute edges with both hands and rock back and forth as if they are rowing, while singing:

Row, row, row your boat,
Gently down the stream,
Merrily, merrily, merrily, merrily,
Life is but a dream.

On the next page is a visualisation which follows on nicely from this activity.

142

75. On the Beach Visualisation

Age Range: 5-11
Ideal Number Of Players: 10+
Equipment Needed: Parachute

What to Do

You can choose to do this visualisation after the song Row, Row, Row Your Boat or just as a calming down exercise at the end of a wet lunchtime.

Ask the players to lie down on the floor under the parachute, close their eyes, get into a comfortable position and relax their bodies. Talk them through the visualisation.

Imagine that you are feeling very sleepy after a day of rowing your boat. Pull the parachute up around you as if you are pulling up your bedclothes ready to go to sleep. You're feeling very sleepy and relaxed.

I'd like you to imagine that you are walking down a beautiful golden sandy beach. You look around you and see children making sandcastles. You hear the sound of the waves in the distance crashing up onto the rocks. You taste the salty sea air and feel the warmth of the sun on your back.

As you wander along the beach you come to a bright yellow deck chair. I'd like you to imagine yourself lying down on this chair. You feel the warmth on your back as you relax into it. You are feeling very calm and peaceful.

Ahead you see a grey misty cloud. I'd like to invite you to place any worries or fears that you have into this cloud. Perhaps you are worried about an aspect of your work, a test, the fact that you've fallen out with a friend. Place those worries into the cloud. You now see this cloud floating higher and higher into the sky to join the other clouds. It starts to get smaller and smaller and becomes as small as a pin prick on the horizon and then it's gone. Now I'd like you to notice how you feel as you sit here on your golden deck chair. Do you feel lighter and happier inside?

I'd now like you to imagine a time when you felt happy inside. It might be when you are playing with your friend or sitting by a fire, or cuddling up reading a book. I'd like to invite you to notice how you feel.

Now I am going to count to ten and you are going to slowly open your eyes, look around the room and smile at someone opposite.

Rules

Players are to keep as still as they can and not distract others.

Variations

You can make up alternative calming down visualisations of your own.

Fruit Salad Cards

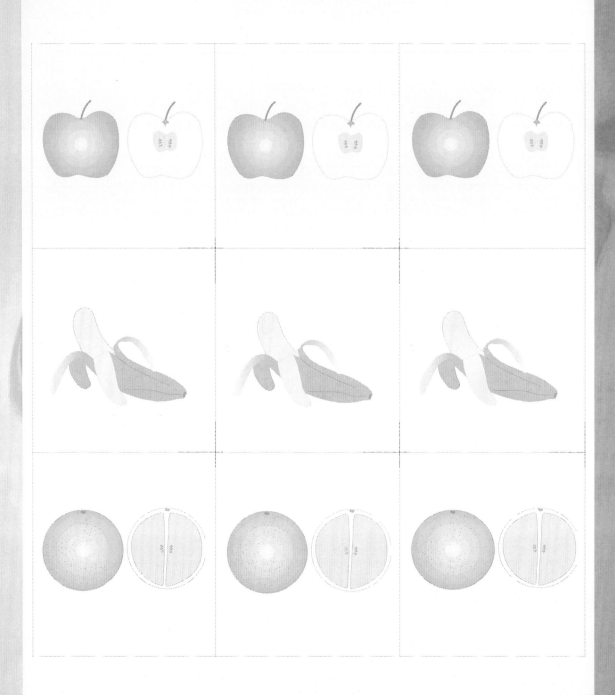

ACTIVE GAMES FOR LETTING OFF STEAM

Active Games for Letting Off Steam

I have chosen to have a section of 'Active Games for Letting off Steam', because we all know that if children aren't given the opportunity to burn off some energy during lunchtime they may choose to do it during lesson time!

There are some fabulous games in this section to fill up your lunch hour. You can choose to play the games in the hall or classroom. The only games that are too active to be played in the classroom are Ladders and Paper, Scissors, Rock.

Paper, Scissors, Rock is a popular two-person hand game, which in this section has been adapted to be played as an active team game.

It is often used as a selection method in a similar way to coin flipping, drawing straws or throwing dice to randomly select a person for playing a game, who's 'on' or some other purpose. However, unlike truly random selections, it can be played with skill if the game extends over many sessions, as a player can often recognise and exploit the non-random behaviour of an opponent.

Sportspeople often use the game, both officially and unofficially, to decide on opening plays.

How to play Paper, Scissors, Rock video

http://www.youtube.com/watch?v=x-QPXcWZ0NI

The People Bingo Game is great for children getting to know each other better.

The Finger and Palm Game involves lots of ducking and diving in an attempt for your partner not to touch your palm. The children love Rock Stars which can be very dramatic! Ha! Ha! Ha! bring lots of laughter and is a gentle feel good game. I love Countdown and play it endlessly on wet play days. The children will need to develop good concentrating, looking and listening skills, so that they can keep the game going.

Enjoy the many games here and have fun!

76. Jacks

Age Range: 7-11
Ideal Number of Players: 1+
Equipment Needed: Set of six Jacks and ball

What to Do

This game is sometimes called Church Stones.

Toss the Jacks on the ground and then toss the ball in the air. Pick up a jack and catch the ball before it hits the ground twice.

After picking up the jacks by ones, do the same with two's, three's, fours, fives and sixes. Children call them onesies, twosies and so on.

Variations

Two other versions of this game are:

1. Use one hand to toss the ball and the other hand to pick up the Jacks.
2. Use the same hand to toss the ball and pick up the Jacks.

In some schools children use stones instead of jacks and with older children they could use coins.

77. Ladders

Age Range: 7-11
Ideal Number of Players: 14+
Equipment Needed: This game should be played in a hall

What to Do

This game can get quite active.

Have the students make two lines. Usually they will have a red and a white team in each class Ask then to get into lines, one line red and one line white.

Ask them to turn so that the two lines are facing each other.

Have them sit down with their legs outstretched in front of them with their feet touching the feet of the person in front of them. Check whether this is culturally acceptable in the country you are teaching in! They have now made a 'ladder' and their feet are the 'rungs' of the ladder.

Assign each pair of students a number. If you have 30 students you will have 15 numbered off.

You then say a number and the pair that are that number race up the ladder around the players and then back down the ladder. The winner is the first player who sits back down in their seat. Teams score a point for the first player back.

The game continues with a new number being chosen.

Rules

Be gentle with one another. Players running up and down the ladder must not tread on others legs.

Variations

An alternative to this is where the teacher takes words out of a story and each player is that word. For example, apple, pear or firework and festival. For 30 students you will need 15 words. You then read a story and every time you say that word the players whose word is mentioned have to race each other.

78. People Bingo

Age Range: 7-11
Ideal Number Of Players: 4+
Equipment Needed: A pencil and copy of the People's Bingo activity page for each player

What to Do

Pass out the People Bingo activity page (page 161).

Players mingle around the group trying to find others who match the descriptions on the sheet. When they find someone who, for example, has a great smile, that person signs the sheet with their name on the dotted line.

The aim of the game is to be the first person with all your boxes signed.

The first player to do this shouts BINGO and is the winner.

Players can keep going until there are several winners.

Rules

People can sign someone's Bingo sheet only once.

79. Make Your Own Bingo

Find someone who:

80. Mirror, Mirror

Age Range: 5-11
Ideal Number of Players: Whole class or 4+
Equipment Needed: Slow, gentle music can be a good idea though is optional

What to Do

This is a good whole-class activity on a rainy day. The players get a good stretch and laugh while reflecting on each others actions.

Pair players up and ask partners to face one another and pretend that they are looking at themselves in a mirror.

One child initiates the action and the other 'mirrors' it.

This works best if the actions are smooth and flowing and partners maintain eye contact. It is helpful if play leaders demonstrate first.

Challenge the players to mirror one another as closely as they can.

Some ideas they can try:
- Making faces at each other – happy, sad, bored, frowning, lifting eyebrows, winking.
- Arm movements – wide sweeping.
- Leg movements – lifts, swinging backwards and forwards.
- Slow and fast movements – sideways, backwards and forwards.

After some practice, have players try imitating each others actions simultaneously, with no designated leader.

Rules

Concentrate as much as you can on each others actions.

Variations

One partner makes up a story mime, for example, combing hair, brushing teeth, putting on a coat, walking out the door, putting up an umbrella.

Small groups mirror the actions of an individual or another group.

81. Rock Star

Age Range: 7-11
Ideal Number of Players: 8+
Equipment Needed: None

What to Do

Ask players to walk around the room and say 'Hello' and shake hands with one another. While shaking hands, the play leader secretly squeezes someone's hand tightly. This person secretly becomes the Rock Star.

As players move around greeting one another, the unidentified Rock Star winks at each player as he shakes hands with them. These players continue as if nothing has happened whilst silently counting to 10. At 10, they gasp and swoon announcing, 'I met a rock star,' and immediately freeze in a position portraying an excited fan.

Anyone not frozen can guess the identity of the Rock Star by saying, 'Rock Star...' and then naming the player. If the guesser is correct the game starts over with a new Rock Star. If not, the guesser freezes in place and the game keeps going. The challenge for the Rock Star is to see how many players he can wink at before being identified by a person within the group.

Variations

In another version of this game you should have two people to challenge the identity of the Rock Star. When someone says, 'Rock Star!' this must be seconded by another player. Then at the count of three, they both say aloud the suspected person's name.

82. The Keeper of the Treasure

Age Range: 5-9
Ideal Number of Players: 8+
Equipment Needed: Keys or a beanbag

What to Do

A suitable treasure is found, for example, a beanbag, set of keys.

The players form a circle and create a space large enough to represent a door for the children to run through.

A leader is chosen. The leader chooses another player to be the keeper of treasure. This player then sits in the middle of the circle with her eyes closed and the treasure placed behind her back.

The leader then silently selects a robber by pointing to a player.

The robber then tip toes as quietly as possible up to the keeper and steals the treasure from behind the keeper's back.

Once the keeper realises the robber has the treasure she leaps to her feet and chases the robber in a clockwise direction around the circle with the intent of catching him. The aim of the game is for either the keeper to catch the robber or for the robber to get back to the keepers home base in the centre of the circle.

While the players wait for the robber to steal the treasure they chant, 'The robber is coming, the robber is coming, the robber is coming,' and then as the robber picks up the treasure and runs out of the door they shout, 'The robber has come!'

If the keeper catches the robber then she is the keeper again, and a new robber is chosen. If the robber gets back to the home base in the centre then he is safe and becomes the keeper and a new robber is chosen.

Rules

If you find when playing this game that players run through gaps in the circle other than the door, it may be helpful at the start of the game to create a rule which says players cannot jump or run out of the windows (the gaps), they can only run out of the door.

154

83. Cornered In

Age Range: 4-11
Ideal Number of Players: 8+
Equipment Needed: Masking tape, blindfold

What to Do

It may sound unbelievable, but standing in a corner can be a lot of fun for children on a rainy day.

Number the four corners of a room using pieces of masking tape stuck to the floor.

Choose one child to be the caller and have her put on a blindfold.

Everybody else forms a circle around the caller.

While the caller quietly counts to ten, the others scurry to corners of their choosing.

The caller shouts out a number from one to four. Whoever is in that corner is out.

Now the caller counts to ten again while the remaining players sneak off to new corners.

The game continues until one person is left. He then becomes the next caller.

84. Ha! Ha! Ha!

Age Range: 5-11
Ideal Number Of Players: 10+
Equipment Needed: None

What to Do

Sometimes called Gigglebelly, Ha! Ha! Ha! is an exercise in the ridiculous.

On the floor, have the children lie down in any formation as long as every child has his head on another child's tummy. The children could form a chain.

At the whistle, the first child you point to should say, 'Ha!' The one whose head is on that child's belly should then say, 'Ha! Ha!' the third should say, 'Ha! Ha! Ha!' and so on.

If you can make it all the way through the line before pandemonium results, you may indeed have a group of professional clowns in your midst.

Rules

If children don't feel comfortable playing this game then they can choose to stay out and watch.

85. Paper, Scissors, Rock

Age Range: 5-11
Ideal Number of Players: 10+
Equipment Needed: Hall to play the game in

What to Do

All players learn the symbols and their meanings:

- Paper = a hand held flat. Paper covers rock, paper wins.

- Scissors = Two fingers, slightly open. Scissors cut paper, scissors win.

- Rock = a closed fist. Rock breaks scissors, rock wins.

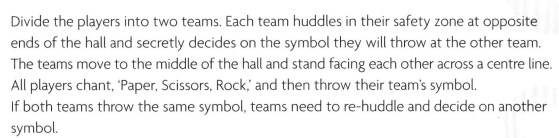

Divide the players into two teams. Each team huddles in their safety zone at opposite ends of the hall and secretly decides on the symbol they will throw at the other team. The teams move to the middle of the hall and stand facing each other across a centre line. All players chant, 'Paper, Scissors, Rock,' and then throw their team's symbol.
If both teams throw the same symbol, teams need to re-huddle and decide on another symbol.
The team that throws the winning symbol chases the other team and tries to tag them before they reach their safety zone.
Players that are tagged, change to the other team. The game ends when all the players are on one team.

Rules

For safety reasons this game needs to be played in a hall.
Before playing, decide on the pace or play, pairing and safe tagging.

Variations

This game can also be played with just two players as a game of just Paper, Scissors, Rock. Children often use this game to select who is going to be 'on' in a game.

86. Countdown

Age Range: 7-11
Ideal Number of Players: 12+
Equipment Needed: None

What to Do

Children sit in a circle either on the floor or on chairs.

A leader is nominated who then goes around the circle counting how many players there are, including himself. That number starts the countdown.

For example, if there were 20 players, the countdown would start from 20. Anyone can stand up and call the next number, 19, but if two children stand up at the same time, the countdown has to start again.

So the play may go something like this, one player stands up and says, '20.' He sits down and then another player stands up and says, '19,' then she sits down and two players stand up to say 18 and the game has to start again.

The aim of the game is to reach 'one' and if they do then all the players stand up, lift their arms and shout, 'Blast off.'

Rules

This game is extremely challenging and requires a lot of concentration. Clearly outline to the children that if two people stand up at any time, then the game starts again. Encourage them to be aware of each others body language. In some instances children will attempt different strategies to succeed, such as saying their numbers in a clockwise fashion around the circle. They soon learn this sort of play isn't much fun and the more sporadic countdown works a lot better.

Variations

Once the children are playing this game confidently, see how quickly they can complete it by using a timer. They may want to compete against themselves beating their previous time.

87. The Finger and Palm Game

Age Range: 7+
Ideal Number of Players: Any number of paired players
Equipment Needed: None

What to Do

Players form pairs and stand facing one another.

Both players hold the palm of their hand flat behind their back whilst with their other hand they use their index finger to point.

Each person attempts to poke their index finger into the palm of their partner's hand, which is of course behind their back and so makes it very difficult.

The aim is to touch their partner's palm and their partner's goal is to make sure that they don't!

Since both players are trying to avoid being poked by their partner there is lots of action with them needing to dip, dodge and move away from their partner.

There are no winners and no losers in this game. It is just great fun and quite exhausting.

Rules

Partner's must stay facing each other

88. The Bean Game

Age Range: 4+
Ideal Number Of Players: 6+
Equipment Needed: None

What to Do

One person is chosen to be the leader

The leader explains the different categories of beans and demonstrates the actions for each.

French Bean – the player says bonjour and bows down.
Jelly Bean – the player wobbles like jelly
Baked Bean – the player lies down on the floor in a stretched out position.
Broad Bean – the player makes a standing starfish shape.
Kidney Bean – the player lies curled up on the floor.
Mexican Bean – the player calls, 'Arribba, aribba, arribba.'

The leader calls a bean and all the players have to do the actions of that bean.

This can be played as a non-competitive game or alternatively competitively with the last child doing the bean action being out. The winner would then be the last person left in.

Variations

This is a game that helps to get rid of lots of excess energy. It is extremely popular with older children and adults love it too!

People Bingo

Has a great smile

....

Is good at listening

....

Sings in the bath or shower

....

Likes to play playground games

....

Loves school

....

Has been on TV

....

Sleeps past 10am on Saturdays

....

Likes to cook

....

Has a funny laugh

....

Has been to more than two countries

....

Plays a musical instrument

....

Is an only child

....

Active Games for Letting Off Steam

SINGING, RHYMES AND DANCING GAMES

Singing, Rhymes and Dancing Games

I have chosen a selection of popular traditional games and rhymes for this section. Many of these have been handed down from generation to generation and would have been known by your parents, grandparents and great grandparents. You may even remember some from your own childhood. I remember singing Ten Green Bottles on a wet play day in my school when I was about seven. It was a game I have really fond memories of. The teachers used to get ten children lining up representing bottles and then every time one bottle fell, a child would fall down. We loved it!

Children love the musical dancing games at the start of this section too. You may know some of these games from parties. They are good energisers and help burn off excess energy.

In and Out the Dusty Bluebells is a very old game and started out as being known as 'Dusky Bluebells'. A long time ago instead of saying, 'Who shall be my partner,' children used to sing, 'Who will be my master.' In fact I remember those days!

'The farmers in his Den' is a very popular game particularly with younger children. In some areas of the country or world 'The Farmers in his Den' is often known as 'The Farmers in his Dell'.

In 'I Sent a Letter to My Love' children have traditionally dropped a hanky, though today they are more likely to carry around paper tissues, which generally wouldn't work as well so alternative suggestions are made. This game is best played in the hall.

The Hokey Cokey is also a game I remember playing on wet play days in our school hall, we also played it at school parties. It tends to be quite raucous and very active. I often find the adults enjoy this one too!

A few of these games have historical significance. 'Ring a Ring a Roses' was attributed to the Black Death/Plague of the 14th century: the 'ring o' roses' was the red rash shaped in a ring which was a symptom of the plague. The 'pocket full o' posies' was the herbs that people carried in an attempt to ward off the disease. 'Atishoo!' was the flu-like symptoms and 'we all fall down' meant that you were dead.

There are many traditional rhymes and games that have a historical background. A great website to check out the origins and meanings of these old rhymes is: www.rhymes.org.uk.

Some ideas for in the classroom are:

- Let the children choose an old singing and dancing rhyme, perhaps one of the above and get them to find out the history, meaning and significance of the words.

- Using the same rhyme, ask them to write new words which fit more with our society and culture today.

- Look at sources such as Wikipedia to research games such as the Hokey Cokey

- YouTube has examples of groups doing some of the games such as the Hokey Cokey.

89. Musical Pairs

Age Range: 3-7
Ideal Number Of Players: 6+
Equipment Needed: Music

What to Do

The players begin by dancing and skipping about the room with the music playing.

When the music stops, everyone takes a partner's hand and they both sit on the floor together. When the music resumes the players skip around together until the music stops once again. Everyone grabs a new partner and the game continues.

If there is an extra player, his first partner can be a stuffed animal, such as a teddy. When the music stops the player sets the bear down and takes a new partner and someone else waltzes off with the 'dancing bear'.

Rules

You can't have the same partner twice.

Variations

Scatter carpet squares or cushions on the floor. When the music stops, partners hurry to find a carpet square to sit on together.

90. Musical Numbers

Age Range: 5-7
Ideal Number of Players: 8+
Equipment Needed: Music

What to Do

A leader is chosen to be a number caller.

All the other players begin dancing and skipping about the room on their own with the music playing.

When the music stops the leader calls out a number to indicate the size of the groups which the players must form. For example, if the leader calls 'five' they have to rush to form a group of five. If he calls 'three' they have to form a group of three. The group must form circles with the right number of players and those not in a circle drop out before the music continues for the next round.

The game continues until only two players are left in the game and they become the two winners.

Rules

Dancing in pairs or groups is not allowed, so keep an eye on those trying to cheat!

91. Musical Statues

Age Range: 4-11
Ideal Number Of Players: 6+
Equipment Needed: Music

What to Do

The players begin by dancing and skipping about the room with the music playing.

When the music stops players have to freeze into 'statues'. As long as the music is off players must hold their statue poses. Anyone who moves or makes a sound is out of the game.

After a few moments the music starts again and the statues come back to life.

Rules

Music should be left off only briefly.

Variations

Play faster music which makes it harder to stay still!
Eliminated players can try to get those left in out, by making faces, telling jokes and so on in the attempt to get those left in to move!

92. In and Out the Dusty Bluebells

Age Range: 5-7
Ideal Number of Players: 8+
Equipment Needed: None

What to Do

The following is a ring dance for at least six dancers.

Verse 1
In and out the dusty bluebells,
In and out the dusty bluebells,
In and out the dusty bluebells,
Who shall be my partner?

Verse 2
Tippity, tappity on your shoulders,
Tippity, tappity on your shoulders,
Tippity, tappity on your shoulders,
You shall be my partner.

Verse 1
Everyone stands in a circle holding their hands up high to make an arch between each dancer. One dancer is chosen and skips in and out of the arches while all players sing the rhyme.

Verse 2
On 'Who shall be my partner' he stops and taps whoever is closest on the shoulder. This dancer then joins onto the first dancer and they weave in and out, again as the first verse is repeated. The game is repeated until all the children form a chain, then they all skip round for as long as they like.

93. The Farmer's in his Den

Age Range: 4-7
Ideal Number Of Players: 8+
Equipment Needed: None

What to Do

The players choose a 'farmer' and then form a circle around him holding hands. They walk in a clockwise direction and chant the following:

The farmer's in his den,
The farmer's in his den.
E...i...e...i,
The farmer's in his den.

This is then repeated with the following words:

The farmer wants a wife,
The farmer wants a wife,
E...i...e...i,
The farmer wants a wife.

The farmer chooses a wife from the circle of children and joins him in the centre. The chant continues with the following verses. After each verse the previously elected child chooses someone from the circle to join the group in the middle.

Verse 3 The wife wants a child.
Verse 4 The child wants a nurse.
Verse 5 The nurse wants a dog.
Verse 6 The dog wants a bone.

The game ends with all players surrounding the child who has been chosen to be the bone. Together they all pat the bone lightly and chant the following:

'We all pat the bone,
We all pat the bone,
E...i...e...I,
We all pat the bone.'

The bone then becomes the 'farmer' and the game begins again.

Rules

When patting the bone, encourage players to be gentle.

94. I Sent a Letter to My Love

Age Range: 5-11
Ideal Number of Players: 6-20
Equipment Needed: An item to use as the letter, an envelope, a handkerchief, hat, glove or similar item

What to Do

Everyone forms a circle, standing or sitting.

One player with a letter (the item) walks or skips around the outside of the circle as the rhyme is chanted.

'I sent a letter to my love
And on the way I dropped it
Someone must have picked it up
And put it in their pocket
It wasn't you, it wasn't you,
It was you!'

As the player says, 'It wasn't you,' he gently taps each player in the circle on the shoulder and repeats, 'It wasn't you,' as many times as he likes with him finally saying, 'It was you!' and dropping the letter on the ground behind the player.

On 'you' the player who has the letter, picks it up and chases the 'letter dropper' around the circle with the aim of catching him.

If the 'letter dropper' gets back into the chasers place without being caught then he is safe and the other player becomes the letter dropper. If she catches the 'letter dropper' he is on again and the game starts again.

Variations

You can substitute 'I sent a letter to my love' with 'I sent a letter to my friend'.

95. The Hokey Cokey

Age Range: 5-11
Ideal Number of Players: 12+
Equipment Needed: None

What to Do

One person is chosen to be a group leader. The players stand in a circle, holding hands. The dance follows the instructions given in the lyrics of the song, which may be prompted by the leader.
You put your right hand in,
Your right hand out,
In, out, in, out,
Shake it all about.
You do the Hokey Cokey and you turn around,
That's what it's all about...

As the specific body parts are named, the players do the appropriate actions.
At the end of each verse the players sing the chorus:

Woah the hokey cokey,
Woah the hokey cokey,
Woah the hokey cokey,
Knees bent arms stretch ra ra ra.

For the chorus all participants stand in the circle. Holding hands, on each 'woah' they all raise their joined hands in the air and run in toward the centre of the circle and on 'the hokey cokey' they all run backwards out again. On the last line they bend their knees then stretch their arms, as indicated, and for 'ra ra ra!' they either clap in time or raise arms above their heads and push upwards in time to the music. More often than not, each subsequent verse and chorus is a little faster and louder.
The next sequence begins with a new named body part and so it continues – left hand, right foot, left foot, whole self.

Rules

Be gentle with one another and make sure nobody gets hurt.

Variations

If you have a large group playing this game and you find it becoming quite boisterous during the chorus, an calmer way of playing, which is almost as much fun, is for the players to raise both their hands up to the side of their head and wiggle their fingers when they sing the chorus.

96. One Man went to Mow

Age Range: 4-6
Ideal Number of Players: 6+
Equipment Needed: None

What to Do

This cumulative playground classic can carry on indefinitely but generally stops at ten men.

The actions include holding up the correct number of fingers, pushing an imaginary mower and patting the dog, Spot. Sometime the children shout 'woof' after the word 'spot'.

One man went to mow,
Went to mow a meadow,
One man and his dog, Spot (woof),
Went to mow a meadow.

Two men went to mow,
Went to mow a meadow,
Two men, one man and his dog, Spot (woof),
Went to mow a meadow.

Three men went to mow,
Went to mow a meadow,
Three men, two men, one man and his dog, Spot (woof),
Went to mow a meadow.

Four men went to mow,
Went to mow a meadow,
Four men, three men, two men, one man and his dog, Spot (woof),
Went to mow a meadow.

The rhyme continues until you reach ten, though sometimes the children like to keep going just for the fun of it!

Variations

Sometimes, the dog's name, Spot, is omitted.

97. Ten Green Bottles

Age Range: 5-11
Ideal Number of Players: 10+
Equipment Needed: None

What to Do

This is a classic game which involves hundreds of green bottles on particularly long wet days or it can be limited to just ten in a short breaktime. The song continues until there are none left. Sometimes the last line of the verse, when only one bottle is left, is sung with merriment. 'There'll be nothing but the smell left hanging on the wall!' accompanied by players holding their noses. The actions include individual children coming to the front and representing green bottles. When one bottle falls a child either falls to the ground or sits down. Alternatively players can hold up fingers for the number of bottles and clap for the word 'fall'.

Ten green bottles hanging on the wall,
Ten green bottles hanging on the wall,
And if one green bottle should accidentally fall,
There'll be nine green bottles hanging on the wall.

Nine green bottles hanging on the wall,
Nine green bottles hanging on the wall,
And if one green bottle should accidentally fall,
There'll be eight green bottles handing on the wall.

Eight green bottles hanging on the wall,
Eight green bottles hanging on the wall,
And if one green bottle should accidentally fall,
There'll be seven green bottles hanging on the wall.

Seven green bottles hanging on the wall,
Seven green bottles hanging on the wall,
And if one green bottle should accidentally fall,
There'll be seven green bottles hanging on the wall.

Six green bottles hanging on the wall,
Six green bottles hanging on the wall,
And if one green bottle should accidentally fall,
There'll be seven green bottles hanging on the wall.

The rhyme continues until there are no green bottles.

174

98. This Old Man

Age Range: 5-11
Ideal Number of Players: 10+
Equipment Needed: None

What to Do

This game is also known as a children's marching song. There are many different ways of performing the actions. In one version the appropriate number of fingers are held up when the number is sung. The words 'knick knack' are accompanied by claps, 'paddy whack' is drummed on any nearby object or on the child's lap and 'rolling home' is accompanied by circular hand movements.

This old man he played one, he played knick knack on my drum,
With a knick knack paddy whack, give the dog a bone, this old man went rolling home.

This old man he played two, he played knick knack on my shoe,
With a knick knack paddy whack give the dog a bone, this old man went rolling home.

This old man he played three, he played knick knack on my knee
With a knick knack paddy whack, give the dog a bone, this old man went rolling home.

This old man he played four, he played knick knack on my door...

This old man he played five, he played knick knack on my hive...

This old man he played six, he played knick knack on my sticks...

This old man he played seven, he played knick knack on my heaven...

This old man he played eight, he played knick knack on my gate...

This old man he played nine, he played knick- knack on my line...

This old man he played ten, he played knick knack on my hen,
With a knick knack paddy whack give the dog a bone, this old man came rolling home.

Rules

Encourage the children to do the actions when singing together.

99. Poor Jenny Stood a Weeping

Age Range: 4-6
Ideal Number Of Players: 8+
Equipment Needed: None

What to Do

Poor Jenny Stood a Weeping is a game that was played in the 1950's and 1960's playground and was often initiated by children themselves. In this game Jenny kneels with her hands to her face 'weeping' while the other children hold hands to form a circle and walk around her as they sing. On the following verse she stands up to her 'sweetheart'. The final verse has the children all skipping around.

Poor Jenny stood a-weeping, a-weeping, a-weeping,
Poor Jenny stood a-weeping, on a bright summers day.
Stand up and choose your loved one, your loved one, your loved one,
Stand up and choose your loved one, on a bright summers day.

And now she is so happy, so happy, so happy,
And now she is so happy, on a bright summers day.

100. Ring a Ring a Roses

Age Range: 4-6
Ideal Number of Players: 6-8
Equipment Needed: None

What to Do

Children form a circle and skip around as they chant the words. On singing 'we all fall down' everyone does just that!

Ring a ring a roses, a pocket full of posies
Atishoo, atishoo, we all fall down.

The King has sent his daughter, to fetch a pail of water,
Atishoo, atishoo, we all fall down.

The birds up on the steeple, sit high above the people,
Atishoo, atishoo, we all fall down.

Variations

There are a variety of different endings to this rhyme. Here are two different versions for you to choose from. In both endings the children jump up on the last line.

1. The cows are in the meadow, eating buttercups,
Atishoo, atishoo, they all jump up.

2. Fishes in the water, fishes in the sea,
We all jump up with a 1, 2, 3.

101. In and Out the Windows

Age Range: 4-6
Ideal Number Of Players: 6-8
Equipment Needed:

What to Do

In the first verse of this game the children stand in a circle and hold hands with their arms raised in an arch. One child is chosen to walk in and out of the arches as the rest of the children chant the rhyme. In following verses the children dance around in a circle singing. In the penultimate verse one child is chosen to stand in the middle, she chooses a sweetheart from the circling children. The 'sweetheart' then joins the child in the circle. For the last verse the two children in the centre join hands and skip.

In and out the window,
In and out the window,
In and out the window,
As we have gone before.

Round and round the levée,
Round and round the levée,
Round and round the levée,
As we have gone before.

Go and find your sweetheart,
Go and find your sweetheart,
Go and find your sweetheart,
As you have done before.

And now you'll both be happy,
And now you'll both be happy,
And now you'll both be happy,
As you have been before.

RESOURCES

Games Template

Name of Game
Age Range:
Ideal Number of Players:
Equipment Needed:

What to Do

Rules

Variations

THE GREAT WET PLAYTIME AWARD

Awarded to:

....

Date

....

Signed

....

THE GREAT WET
PLAYTIME CLASS AWARD

Awarded to:

....

Date

....

Signed

....

CERTIFICATE FOR PLAYING KINDLY

Awarded to:

....

THANK YOU!

Date

....

Signed

....

STAR CHILD

○○○

STAR PLAYER

○○

CAUGHT BEING GOOD

○○

WONDERFUL BEHAVIOUR DURING WET PLAYTIME

A GREAT TEAM PLAYER

A TREMENDOUS HELP DURING WET PLAYTIME TODAY. THANK YOU

RAINBOW ACTIVITY LEADER AWARD

This is to certify that:

....

has successfully completed a programme of supervising activities during wet playtimes.

Awarded to:

THANK YOU!

Date

....

Signed

....

Appendix

Puzzles

School Discovery Education has an amazing resource called Puzzlemaker where children can create their own puzzles online.

http://puzzlemaker.discoveryeducation.com/

Puzzle Games by Debbie

www.debidawn.com

This is a wonderful website filled with puzzle games for everyone. It includes Wordsearch Puzzles, Crossword Puzzles, Kris Kross, Jigsaw Puzzles, Fun and Easy Word Search for Kids, Dot-to-Dots, Crosswords for Kids, Mazes.

Debbie regularly adds new activities.

Another puzzle website, with a wealth of puzzle options for children

http://www.puzzlechoice.com/pc/Kids_Choicex.html

www.games.co.uk

Quiz Websites

http://www.triv.net/html/Quiz6/quiz264.shtml

http://www.quiz.co.uk/kids/animals1/

http://www.quiz.co.uk/kids/animals2/

http://www.quizland.com/kidsonly.mv

Thinking Games

Noughts and crosses web based games

http://www.noughtsandcrosses.org/

http://www.wirral-mbc.gov.uk/onlinegames/osandxs/osandxs.asp

http://www.machinehead-software.co.uk/misc/tic_tac_toe/index.html

Hangman

http://www.hangman.no/

http://www.hangman.learningtogether.net/

Sudoku

Web Sudoku – Billions of Free Sudoku Puzzles to Play Online

There are a vast variety of websites with Sudoku games. Here are just a few website, for a variety of ability levels.

http://www.websudoku.com/

http://www.activityvillage.co.uk/sudoku_for_kids.htm

Origami

http://dev.origami.com/diagram.cfm

http://www.origami-club.com/en/

http://www.origamiwithrachelkatz.com/index.html

http://www.oriland.com/index.asp

Death Masks

http://www.liverpoolmuseums.org.uk/nof/top/deathmask.html

Rangoli

For more ideas go to: http://www.activityvillage.co.uk/rangoli.htm

Improvisation Games

http://improvencyclopedia.org/games/index.html

Music

http://www.broadchart.com/Playtime/PThome.htm

Other Resources

Wet Games Mats

These mats contain fun activities for wet playtimes, choosing time or spare minutes in class. Place the mats back to back before laminating. Pupils could use whiteboard pens and wipe the mats clean afterwards, so they can be used time and time again. Keep your pupils engaged whilst reinforcing literacy and numeracy http://www.top-teaching-tools.com/Resources/Primary/Classroom%20Management/WetPlaytimes/index.html

Are you bored during breaktimes? Then try out these links and get rid of your wet playtime blues. Remember to ask your teacher for permission.

http://www.yahooligans.com/

http://www.exploratorium.edu/

http://www.xtramsn.co.nz/kids/

http://www.ashurst.st-helens.sch.uk/pupilresource/wetplaygames.htm

http://www.amblesideprimary.com/ambleweb/wetplay.htm

http://www.hellinglyschool.co.uk/Wet%20Play.php

Survey's

Survey monkey – http://www.surveymonkey.com/

Survey gizmo – https://www.surveygizmo.com

Other Useful Websites

Play Equipment

Edventure

Tel: 01323 501040

http://www.edventure.co.uk

Email: sales@edventure.co.uk

Edventure is a major supplier of playtime games to two thirds of all UK primary schools.

They specialise in the design, manufacture, and supply of playtime games to schools throughout the UK. Edventure was formed by a retiring head teacher who believed that it was important to encourage children to play games in the playground at playtimes for the improvement of social skills and behaviour.

Parachute Distributors

SeamStress Ltd

23 Banbury Road

Byfield

Northants

Tel: 01327-263933

www.playchutes.com

info@playchutes.com

This company makes each parachute to your colour and size specifications.

Sportswarehouse – http://www.sportswarehouse.co.uk/ (sell well- priced parachutes).

Bee-Tee Products Ltd, Cemetery Lane, Carlton, Wakefield, West Yorkshire WF3 3QT.

Organisations

Children's Play Council

c/o National Children's Bureau

8 Wakely Street

London EC1V 7QE

Tel. 020 7843 6016

E-mail: cpc@ncb.org.uk

Children's Play Information Service. The Play Council produces informative newsletters.

Play England

Children's Play Council

8 Wakley Street

London EC1V 7QE

Tel: 020 7843 6300

Website: http://www.playengland.org.uk/

Play England's aim is for all children and young people in England to have regular access and opportunity for free, inclusive, local play provision and play space.

Play England provides advice and support to promote good practice, and works to ensure that the importance of play is recognised by policy makers, planners and the public.

V&A Museum of Childhood

Cambridge Heath Road

London E2 9PA

United Kingdom

Tel: +44 (0)20 8983 5200

Fax: +44 (0)20 8983 5225

Email: moc@vam.ac.uk

Website: http://www.vam.ac.uk/moc/index.html

Organisations Running Playtime Programmes and Games Training

Powerfully Positive Playtimes Programme

A whole-school approach to creating positive and harmonious playtimes.

Training available in the UK, New Zealand, Australia and Pacific Region.

E mail: play@thesuccesspartnership.org

Web site: www.thesuccesspartnership.org

Books with More Ideas for Games, Play and Creativity

Good Practice in Playwork by Paul Bonel, Jennie Lindon. Stanely Thornes Ltd, Cheltenham.

Great Games to Play with Groups: A Leaders Guide, Frank Harris. A Teacher-Aid Book, Fearon, Illinois.

Games, Games, Games, by Rachael Dewar, Kate Palser, Martin Notley, Andy Piercy. Woodcraft Folk, London.

Let's Cooperate, Mildred Masheder. Green Print, London.

Let's Play together: 300 Cooperative Games by Mildred Masheder. Green Print, London.

Parachute Games by Lorraine Barbarash. Human Kenetics, Leeds.

Parachute Games with DVD by Todd Strong and Dale N. Le Fevre. Human Kinetics, Leeds.

The Spirit of Play by Dale N. Le Fevre. Findhorn, Scotland.

The Good Childhood Inquiry

The Good Childhood Inquiry is the UK's first independent national inquiry into childhood. The inquiry is seeking to open an inclusive debate on what makes for a good childhood today that will shape future policy and inspire all our relationships with children.

The Children's Society has commissioned a series of public opinion polls, called 'Reflections on Childhood' as part of The Good Childhood Inquiry. You can read the six polls on:

1. Friends

http://www.childrenssociety.org.uk/resources/documents/good%20childhood/Reflections%20on%20Childhood%20Friendship_3189_full.pdf

2. Family

http://www.childrenssociety.org.uk/resources/documents/good%20childhood/Reflections%20on%20Childhood%20Family_3191_full.pdf

3. Learning

http://www.childrenssociety.org.uk/resources/documents/good%20childhood/Reflections%20on%20Childhood%20Learning_3193_full.pdf

4. Lifestyle

http://www.childrenssociety.org.uk/resources/documents/good%20childhood/6293_full.pdf

5. Health

http://www.childrenssociety.org.uk/resources/documents/good%20childhood/7082_full.pdf

6. Values

http://www.childrenssociety.org.uk/resources/documents/good%20childhood/7629_full.pdf

Bibliography

Almond, J. & Hallan, V. (1995) *Training Manual for Lunchtime Supervisors*. Walsall. Birmingham: UK Equal Opportunities Unit.

Augarde, T. (2003) *The Oxford Guide to Word Games*. Oxford: Oxford University Press.

Bason, S. (2009) *Learning Outside the Classroom*. London: Teach to Inspire, Optimus Education.

Bishop, J. C. & Curtis, M. (2001) Play Today in the Primary School Playground. Buckinghamshire: Open University Press.

Blatchford, P. & Sharp, S. (2005) *Breaktime and the School: Understanding and Changing Playground Behaviour*. London: Routledge.

Blatchford, P. & Baines, E. (2008) *The Social and Educational Significance of School Breaktimes*. Seminar briefing paper, 29th April. England. The Nuffield Foundation.

Blatchford, P. & Baines, E. (2006) *A Follow-Up National Survey of Breaktimes in Primary and Secondary Schools*. Report to Nuffield Foundation. Psychology and Human Development, Institute of Education, London and The Nuffield Foundation. Ref: EDV/00399/G.

Brandes, D. & Phillips, H. (1995) *Gamesters' Handbook*. Philideliphia, USA: Trans-Atlantic Publishing.

Broadhead, P. (2004) *Early Years Play and Learning: Developing Social Skills and Cooperation*. London: Routledge Press.

De Bono, E. (1992) *Serious Creativity*. New York: Harper Business.

DFES (2005) *Excellence and Enjoyment: Social and Emotional Aspects of Learning*. London: DfES.

DFES(2004) *Every Child Matters: Change for children in school*. London: DfES.

Dishman, R. K. http://www.getcited.org/mbrz/11058686,

http://www.getcited.org/inst/142760

Seefeldt, V. (1986) *Physical Activity & Wellbeing*. American Alliance for Health, Physical Education, Recreation and Dance. USA.

http://www.getcited.org/pub/102591712

Frost, J., Wortham, S. & Reifel, S. (2005) *Play and Child Development*. Upper Saddle River, New Jersey: Merrill/Prentice Hall.

Gill, T. (2007) *No Fear: Growing Up in a Risk-Averse Society*. London: Calouste Gulbenkian Foundation.

A number of his articles are available online. See: http://www.rethinkingchildhood.com/

Goleman, D. (1995) *Emotional Intelligence. Why it matters more than IQ*. London: Bloonmsbury.

Goleman, D. (2007) *Social Intelligence. The new science of human relationships*. London: Arrow Books Ltd.

Henig, R. M. (2008) 'Taking Play Seriously', 17th February. *The New York Times*: New York.

Holden, R. (1993) *Laughter the Best Medicine*. London: Harper Collins.

Hoyle, T. (2008) *101 Playground Games*. London: Teach to Inspire. Optimus Education.

Johnson, J. E., Christie, J. F. & Wardle, F. (2005) *Play, Development and Early Education*. Boston, MA: Pearson Education.

Le Fevre, D. N. (2007) *The Spirit of Play*. Scotland: Findhorn Press.

Le Fevre, D. N. (2006) *Parachute Games*. Leeds: Human Kinetics.

Hoyle, T. (2008) *101 Playground Games*. London: Teach to Inspire. Optimus Education.

Kane, P. (2005) *The Play Ethic: A Manifesto for a Different Way of Living*. London: Pan Books.

Lester, S. & Russell, W. (2007 & 2008) 'Play for a Change', Play England:

http://www.playengland.org.uk/Page.asp?originx_1942ye_79921990808192u23p_2008331333u

http://www.playengland.org.uk/play/play-for-a-change-briefing.pdf

Masheder, M. (1997) *Let's Play Together*. Guilford: Green Print.

MacConville, R. (2009) *Teaching Happiness*. London: Teach to Inspire, Optimus Education.

McGonigal, Jane. (2007) *'McGonigal Vanguard Tti Altrealities*, *July,*

Showme:

http://www.slideshare.net/avantgame/mc-gonigal-vanguard-tti-altrealities-july2007-showme?from=email&type=share_slideshow&subtype=slideshow

Naisbitt, J. (1984) *Megatrends*. New York: Warner Books.

National Union of Teachers (2007) *Time to Play*. London: NUT.

Opie, I. & Opie, P. (1969) *Children's Games in Street and Playground*. London: Oxford University Press.

Panksepp, J. (1993) 'Rough and Tumble Play: A Fundamental Brain Process'. In MacDonald, K. B. (Ed.) *Parents and Children Playing*. Albany, NY: Suny Press.

Panksepp, J. & Ikemoto, S. (1992) 'The effects of early isolation on motivation for social play in juvenile rats'. *Developmental Psychbiology*, May, 24(4): p261-74.

Patte, M. M. (2006) 'What's Happened to Recess: Examining Time Devoted to Recess in Pennsylvania's Elementary Schools', in *Play & Folklore* (October), no.48, p.6.

Sharp, S. & Smith, P. (1991-1993) Tackling Bullying: The Sheffield Project in understanding and managing bullying. Oxford: Heinemann Educational.

Siraj-Blatchford, I. & Sylva, K. (2004) 'Researching Pedagogy in English Pre-Schools', *British Education Journal*, 30 (5), p713- 730.

Smith, P. K. & Sharp, S. (eds) (1994) *School Bullying: Insights and Perspectives*. London: Routledge.

Sunderland, M. (2006) *The Science of Parenting.* London: Dorling Kindersley.

Sutton–Smith, B. (2003) 'Play as a Parody of Emotional Vulnerability', in Roopnarine, J. L. (ed) *Play and Educational Theory and Practice, Play and Culture Studies 5.* Westport, Connecticut.

The Children's Society (2007) Good Childhood Inquiry – What you told us about friends. http://www.childrenssociety.org.uk/all_about_us/how_we_do_it/the_good_childhood_inquiry/1818.html

Wenner, M. (2009) *The Serious Need to Play.* USA: Scientific American Mind.

Wood, E. & Atfield, J. (2005) Play, Learning and the Early Childhood Curriculum (2nd Edition). London: Paul Chapman.

Wood, E. (2007) *New Directions in Play: Consensus or Collision?* Cambridge: Routledge. Education 3-13 Vol.35, No. 4, November 2007, p309-320.

Games Index